Key West
Conch Smiles

A Native's Collection of
Legends, Stories, Memories
by
Jeane Porter

Published by **Mancorp Publishing**
P. O. Box21492, Tampa, FL 33622

Library of Congress Cataloging-in-Pulication Datta

Porter, Jeane, 1926-
    Key West conch smiles: a native's collection of legends,
  stories, memories / by Jeane Porter
      p. cm.
    Includes bibliographical references.
    ISBN 0-931541-64-6
    1. Key West (Fla.)-- Biography--Anecdotes. 2. Key West
(Fla.)--social life and customs--Anecdotes. 3. Porter, Jeane,
1926-- Anecdotes. 4. Porter, Jeane, 1926- --Family--Anecdotes.
5. Porter family--Anecdotes. 6. Celebrities--Florida--Key West-
Anecdotes. I. Title
F319.K4P67   1998
920.0759'41--dc21
[B]   98-25156
                                                                                    CIP

410 Caroline Street, Key West, Florida 33040
Phone: 305-296-3573

Manufactured in the United States of America

ISBN 0-931541-64-6

DEDICATION

*I dedicate this offering to the very special people of
Key West who have enriched the past, to my children;
Porter, Renée & Suzanne and to my grandsons Kieran
and Kyle who light up the future.*

With Grateful Appreciation and thanks to:

Alberto De Andrea, *Robert Frost illustration*
Robert Bender, Creative Services, *graphic troubleshooting*
Suzanne Campbell, *general support & photographs*
Margretta Campbell, *technical help*
Dennis Cooper, Key West, the Newspaper, *publishing*
Bob Compton, *encouragement and egging me on*
Suzie Depoo, *Mermaid and Cock drawings*
Marianne Duchardt, Monroe County Public Library, reference assistant
Jack Dudley and Alice Dudley Breedon, *woodblock artist, WPA period*
Frank Fernandez, Cuban Leaf Cigar Factory – Porter House, 429 Caroline Street
Judith Gaddis, Heritage House Museum, director
Adolph Gucinski, *photo restoration*
Caren Hoth, *library research assistance*
Tom and Linda Hambright, Florida Room, Monroe County Public Library
Nancy 3. Hoffman, *editing and historical research*
Colin G. Jameson, *editorial assistance*
Cynthia Lawson, Monroe County Public Library, *assistance*
Wallace Kirke, *drawings of Key West*
George LaPointe, Heritage House, *historical art and photo research*
Luz Marina, *secretarial assistance*
Bridgett McDonald, *copy-editing and editorial assistance*
Margaret Muir, *copy-editing*
Sarah Miller, *sustenance*
Benjamin Peskoe, *copy-editing and editorial assistance*
Porter Poirier, *love and encouragement*
John Stewart, *financial advise*
Bob Tucker, Radio Shack, *technical help*
Martha Watson Sauer, *illustrations – Key West woodblocks*

And not to forget Jessie Porter Newton and Grace Dorgan Porter,
who told many of these stories to me.

TABLE OF CONTENTS

BACKGROUND MUSIC

FAMILY AND FRIENDS

HEMINGWAY

POP - WILLIAM RANDOLPH PORTER

BIG MAMA GRACE DORGAN PORTER

KEY WEST PERSONALITIES

OLD KEY WEST

OLD FAMILY STORIES

MISS JESSIE

FAMILY HELPERS

Background Music

Confessions
Jessie Porter Newton
Champions for Breakfast
Livestock
Family Wisdoms

A delicate balance
W.R. Porter, Jessie & Grace in the far, far West.

Confessions

There is no doubt that history in some perverse and mischievous way often does repeat itself. Friends have asked me many times to collect and write down stories and family memoirs, some of them from generations back. I have felt flattered by this suggestion, but as my grandmother, Grace Porter must have felt before me, when people would exclaim after hearing one of her stories, "Oh, Mrs. Porter, that story was wonderful! Why don't you write?"

Big Mama would always laugh and answer, "Because I would so much rather have people say, "Oh, Mrs. Porter, why don't you write?" than, "Oh, Mrs. Porter, why DID you write?"

As I am now quite high up on that ladder into the next universe, I feel many of these stories belong not just to me exclusively, but to Key West and the larger world as well. So I am putting aside my grandmother's good example and plunging into waters that feel both warm and inviting. I hope you will enjoy them with me.

People always assume since I am a sixth generation Conch (pronounced Konk), a native Key Wester, that I was born here in

St. Paul's Episcopal Church, Duval St.

Key West. If they try to pin me down to the "actually factual and factually actual" (one of Mother's favorite expressions), I answer as matter-of-factly as is factually possible that I was born on January 4, 1926, in Bronxville, New York, because I wanted to be near my mother. This is an answer that seems to quiet and satisfy everyone.

However, kind Fate, with the help of my parents, brought me down to Key West a month later on the wonderful Florida East Coast Railroad — to the waiting arms of loving and eager grandparents, Grace and Will Porter. I was baptized at St. Paul's Episcopal Church on Duval Street, which proved to be an unusually useful happening. Somehow my birth certificate became lost, and the baptismal records were all that I had to identify me officially as part of this world. They later helped to secure my first passport to go to Europe to study art.

I was born a Capricorn, a workaholic who adores to wake up in the morning knowing I have something useful and creative to do. Most of my life I have considered myself a painter, and still do, but one who also likes to write.

It has often been said that you can take the Conch out of Key West, but not Key West out of the Conch — at least not for long. In 1956 I married a geologist, Art Poirier, and had three children, Porter and Renee, a "pigeon pair," born in Australia in '57 and '58, and Suzanne, born in '62 in Paris. We moved professionally to various parts of the globe: from Australia to Paris to the Hague, to Connecticut, to California, and finally Madagascar — an exciting life. In 1979, I returned to Key West permanently, following my mother's death, to pick up the reins of family property management. Key West has gone through so many upheavals and transformations in its rollercoaster past — wars, fires, yellow fever outbreaks, hurricanes, loss of the cigar and sponge industries, wrecking and depressions — all this and survived. Its latest "high," its success as a world tourist attraction, may be the biggest threat of all to its survival and identity. It is primarily for that reason that my family and I have preserved 410 Caroline Street as Heritage

Jeane's children: Suzanne, Porter, and Rene
Seventh Generation Key Westers

House Museum. Each period of Key West history is represented and alive and well in this house. After all, we already have the "sets and costumes and characters."

Growing up in the Old South means that I was reared and weaned on adages to live by, a form of illustrated teaching that has fallen by the wayside in current education. The fact that they often included humor as well as wisdom was an extra dividend. Many of the stories contained in this collection are ones that my mother, my grandmother and older relatives and friends told me, that have helped to fashion my life.

I used to think that my grandmother's wisdom; "Good manners get you further and cost you less than anything else in the world", was too manipulative and calculating. But I have changed my mind completely about this. The current world lacks much in grace and style that it once had, that I believe must be recaptured and/or created anew. Good manners are the oil that lubricates and keeps the social wheels turning without too much friction, overheating or burning up, and as Miss Jessie said, "Courtesy, after all, really is kindness in dress clothing."

In relating these stories and memoirs, I believe each of us is a repository of time and the culture we have lived in. This, like most artifacts, tells a story, paints a picture and saves a part of, hopefully, what is valuable and useful, decorative and fun. Our memories are the furniture of our psyche. I want to invite friends in to sit and share with me what I can salvage that isn't too damaged or too fragile; To speak, and when I speak, to really SAY something, (see the story "Mammy").

* * *

And as the old African Bushman said, "We are all as old as our deepest griefs and as young as our wildest dreams."

Heritage House Museum 410 Caroline Street photo by Dr. Alex Caemmerer from his book "The Houses of Key West". Alex is a psychiatrist – his subjects seem to know this and respond and reveal themselves to his lens in a special way. Heritage House is a classic example of a ships carpenter – Caribbean Sea Captain's house. Capt. George Carey first built a smaller version in 1836 but moved it to the rear when he became a successful spirits dealer in 1838 and added this larger addition in front.

Jessie Porter Kirke Newton, porch communing – 1965

Jessie Porter Newton and Heritage House

Just as an artist uses paint and canvas, Miss Jessie's medium was people. She was a Past Master and loved to combine old friends and new acquaintances socially together to create anything but "Still Life." Heritage House and Gardens at 410 Caroline Street was her canvas and her gatherings were her masterpieces.

Miss Jessie was a fifth generation Key Wester, with many of the Island's notables and contributive personalities as her forebearers: John Lowe, the master wrecker; Captain Thomas Mann Randolph, Commander of the early Coast Guard following Commodore David Porter's anti-piratical fleet; William Curry, ships' chandler and financier and Florida's first millionaire, were her great-great and great grandfathers. Her grandfather was Dr. Joseph Yates Porter, a pioneer in preventative medicine and the first director of the Florida State Board of Health, one of the first such boards in the country. Dr. Porter is credited with eradicating yellow fever. Her father was William Randolph Porter, Key West developer, owner and president of the bank that for over forty years sustained Key West's economy before, during the depth of the Great Depression and after.

Miss Jessie, as she was affectionately called, was a diminutive (five foot three) dynamo of creative and hereditary energy. In 1930, she and my father, Wallace Kirke, returned to Key West, he with a serious heart condition. Early on they recognized the unique architectural value of Key West's sea carpenters' houses (West Indian Colonial), and their vulnerability to being destroyed. They acquired 410 Caroline Street (Heritage House) located then in the midst of other family residences. It was in terrible condition, but they lovingly restored it themselves with the aid of the gifted black carpenter Joe Hannibal. In this period, the 1930s, Miss Jessie is credited with collecting the funds that were matched by the government to create the Aquarium, starting the Flower Show (see the story "All First Prizes"), and, with Pauline Hemingway and Katie dos Passos, launching The Old Island Trading Post as a shop that developed and sold native handcrafts during the deep Depression. Lilly Daché, world famous hat designer visiting here, got her inspiration from the straw hats made locally for this fascinating shop.

Miss Jessie's gatherings to promote Key West were legendary, bringing together currents of creativity and influence from all over the world. Through Heritage House's hospitable doors have flowed many of the powerful people of the twentieth century. From admirals to artists, from poets to dancers, from politicos to pundits, such was the rich and varied life and attraction of the Island and of its leading hostess.

Miss Jessie was the originator of The Old Island Restoration Foundation, that first began its meetings in Heritage House gardens. Old Island Days, an annual celebration of historic Key West, was Jessie's brainchild, along with "red shawling" and the Old House and Garden Tours – Heritage House being the first to be shown. She was also instrumental in saving the Audubon House, Wreckers' House and hundreds of houses on the island.

The poet Robert Frost, an old friend and admirer of Miss Jessie's, spent many winters visiting Key West and stayed in the Heritage House garden cottage, now named in his honor (see "Frost in the Garden"). Their mutual friends, the philosopher John Dewey, the poets Wallace Stevens and Archibald MacLeish, the writer Thornton Wilder, and many others, enjoyed relaxing and talking together under the spell of this exotic old garden (see the chapter "Family and Friends").

Heritage House is a celebration of Key West's most colorful and contributing individuals, and the Island's most turbulent and exciting history. Its interior contains unique pieces, objects d'art and mementos from all of the Island's past, from Chinese reverse paintings given as gifts to the Porter family by their friend the premiere Florida visionary and developer Henry Flagler (see "All Aboard!"), to Dr. Mudd's shell box, made while he was still a prisoner at Fort Jefferson, after his conviction as part of the conspiracy that assassinated President Lincoln. Many of the furnishings are from Key West's halcyon days of wrecking, salvaged by family ancestors. Objects from China and East Indian trade are highlighted. Others are from both the Civil War and the Spanish American War, and include WWI and WWII, when Key West was once again thrust into the active center of national defense, this time as the center of anti-German U-boat warfare (see "Presidential Cracks" and "World War II").

The first owner and builder of the house (1836-38) was a jaunty Englishman, Captain George Carey, who made his fortune in the wholesale and retail spirit (liquor) business. The house was surveyed and documented by the Historic American Buildings Survey and is considered a classic of the West Indian Colonial-Sea Carpenter architecture at its best.

Interiors:
Heritage House, 410 Caroline Street
photos by Suzanne Campbell

Joe Hannibal and "Baby"
Playing in the Garden

William Randolph Porter c.1950
"Pop"

Champions for Breakfast

reakfast with my grandfather, William R. Porter was always an exciting adventure; a little like going into the proverbial lion's den; risky and emotionally dangerous but challenging and always full of generously shared booty and treats. Sometimes, it was also High Theater.

Pop, as I called him lovingly (a not uncommon title in the old South as was Big Mama and Big Daddy), was a patriarch, a financier, an autocrat, a Taurus, a widower, a gourmet and now a newly retired bank president. He had held the economic reins of the Island for over twenty five years with the only bank that didn't fold before or during the Depression. His leisurely retirement breakfasts had become sumptuous adventures. They began with fruit of the season: melons or mangoes or sugar apples or papayas from his "rock garden," often followed by crisp smoked Canadian bacon or sausages flanking hominy grits, which were called "hatracks for gravy" by the Old South. This was often served with delicious Spanish omelets or Shad roe scrambled with eggs, or sometimes lamb fricassee. We often enjoyed the classic Key West breakfast, grits and grunts: a local pan-fried fish that grunted when caught. Pop considered the crème-de-la-crème of fish to be broiled Pompano and Moon fish, a rare delicacy. Moon fish were a flat round silvery fish eight to ten inches in diameter. When deep fried they became completely edible from head to crispy tail, and delicious beyond words. Any or all of this bounty was often embellished by Sophie's home-made buttermilk biscuits or her light and golden Sally Lunn bread. I'll never forget breakfasts with Pop.

One breezy morning in March, I hurried around the corner of Caroline and headed up Duval to his house just beyond my great-grandfather Dr. Porter's house on the corner. A small crowd was gathered there. Something unusual was brewing in the wind and about to happen. I sensed it but I was already running ten minutes late for breakfast and feared the consequences. My grandfather was not one to be kept waiting by anyone, least of all by me. I entered the side porch door of the double living rooms and hurried through the large rambling Victorian house to the airy dining room in its center and heart. Pop was already seated at the head of the massive oak dining table, enthroned in his high backed armchair.

He was a short, stocky man, not more than five feet seven or eight, but his robust frame, energetic movements and portly banker's front, always dressed in immaculate white linen, gave him a volume and edge of energy and power that was very impressive. His hair parted in the center, circa 1920, was gray and wavy above a broad, high forehead. Depending on his mood, his eyes could be either amused or menacing behind wire framed glasses mounted on a roller coaster nose that had once been almost straight and noble. I feel I have inherited the female version of his

President Truman's Little White House – Key West

"The Little White House"
- notice the radio tower in the background

square jaw and stubborn chin and probably some of his vesuvian temperament as well.

It was late March, tax-paying time, and Pop's mood this morning was well along a mined road set for an explosion. He greeted me with a booming, sarcastic but not unfriendly, "Well, here is the late Miss Jeane," and then continued inquiringly and with a mixture of suspicion and concern. "Couldn't sleep worth a tinker's damn last night," he growled, "and I could see your balcony lights were on until it was well after midnight!"

He squinted speculatively over at me. The second floor windows at the back of his 1897 Victorian house commanded a long view to the third floor of our old sea captain house around the corner on Caroline Street. 410's third floor balcony apartment, which I had occupied since returning home from college (I was now about twenty-two), could be seen from his back bedroom. This high-up third floor perch floated over the tropical gardens below like a magic carpet over a leafy sea. I loved my world up there that my father had created for me by converting the attic into an apartment. It had been a Christmas gift when I was thirteen. On hot summer nights the balcony doors could be opened wide to a skyfull of cascading stars. It was a truly romantic spot.

I tried not to sound defensive, and answered cautiously, "Yes, Pop, I did have a few friends over — it was such a hot night that we sat out on the balcony and talked, and I played the guitar and sang. We didn't realize that it had become so late."

"Hrumph," responded my grandfather, his own exuberant youth no doubt flooding back to him in a wave of envy. "In my day and age," he growled, "if I were with a young woman until after midnight . . . I wouldn't have been there taking singing lessons!'" Pop always suspected his progeny of being as wayward and wicked as the 'sinner' he considered himself to be.

I laughed nervously. "Well, your day and age was so much more romantic than mine," I admitted ruefully. "We just sing and talk most of the time now." I wouldn't have misbehaved for anything under my parents' roof — except to smoke, and that I did secretly.

I sensed that Pop's rapacious mood was sporting for a fight. To deflect it, I began to talk about the city commission's and Mayor Harvey's recent decision to rename Division Street, Truman Avenue, in honor of the President while he was still in town. The city at large outwardly had accepted the name change gracefully, being too polite to protest while the President was still on the Island. Truman had just won the national election against Dewey to the country's amazement, and had returned to Key West to celebrate his victory . . . it had become his holiday ritual. He and his family and cabinet members and guests occupied both the Commandant's and the Executive Officer's Quarters in the Navy yard near us. Those quarters were beginning to be called "The Little White House" by the national and international press. It was wonderful worldwide publicity for Key West, and the town was grateful for it and to him, though many people weren't that terribly wild about Harry then.

Every morning from our front porch we could see Truman in brightly flowering Hawaiian sport shirts, a new holiday fashion, walking at a terrific clip out of the Presidential Gates on Whitehead Street, past our house on Caroline. He was always accompanied by two or three secret service men valiantly huffing and puffing to keep up and abreast of him. Meanwhile, during the day, Mrs. Truman would often go shopping at Mother's fascinating Old Island Trading Post gift shop just outside the Gates. Bess loved shopping, especially for tea cups and saucers to add to her collection. Her daughter Margaret would often be in tow.

"Imagine," said Opal, Jessie's attractive friend and manager of the shop. "She tried to haggle the price down from just five dollars for a cup and saucer. It's Staffordshire bone china, too! So I said, 'Oh, Mrs. Truman, won't you please accept these as a gift! It would be our pleasure to give them to you.'"

"A gift?" laughed Jessie. "That was a mistake Opal!" She just loves to barter. Next time she comes in and wants to haggle, lower the price to three — but don't ever give anything away to her. It will make her day if you just come down in price."

The Navy Commandant, Captain Crenshaw, and his second in command, whose quarters the President occupied with his party, had learned to bunk in lesser quarters on the base and settle in for the blow with a grin-and-bear-it stoicism. After all, who, as a lowly Captain, could you complain or send a bill to after a Presidential visit when your Commander and Chief and his party drank up all your liquor supply? Certainly not the War Department!

"I was talking with my friend Alice, the Commandant's daughter," I told Pop, hoping to entertain and distract him. "She said that the President and his party are having a really grand old time of it. She said that they are whooping it up, drinking and playing poker every night — all night. She said we should hear him playing the piano. He's not bad!"

This was too much. Pop exploded like the wounded Southern Taxpaying Autocrat that he was. "That son of a sea cook haberdasher!" he roared. "He's no better than FDR became with all his giveaway programs. He's bankrupting this country, squandering hard-earned money to baby and coddle every one of our enemies. He's ruining this country!"

By now, I had finished my melon and had begun sampling the highly seasoned and delicious Spanish omelet as he fumed. I could feel both my inner and outer sensibilities being warmed simultaneously, an interesting sensation. In the early 20s, Pop had met and had often entertained FDR when, as Assistant Secretary of the Navy, he had come down to Key West to conduct business as well as relax and fish. With the disastrous evacuation of the cigar industry to Tampa and the destruction of the sponge beds by blight, economic depression had come much earlier to Key West than to the rest of the U.S with its stock market crash in 1929. The only glue that held the Island together economically was Norburg Thompson's fishing and canned turtle soup businesses and my grandfather's First National Bank.

Pop's worries for the economic future of Key West and its survival were devastating and had weighed heavily on his shoulders for years. So, immediately after Roosevelt's election as president, it was he who as a Roosevelt supporter and as the Island's only surviving banker, had high-tailed it up to Washington to persuade Roosevelt to try out his New Deal plans in Key West. "We're an island with natural boundaries," he reminded FDR. "You can try out your plans to unique advantage here, and see how and if they work."

Jeane Porter Kirke – 1948

Roosevelt had agreed and sent his youngest administrator, Jules Stone, to begin the FERA and WPA projects here. Though the Conchs are a tough and resilient bunch, the Island could have gone under economically had there not been this government rescue. Roosevelt's New Deal concepts, on the whole, worked and multiplied, spreading all over the U.S.

Suddenly the sound of a military band came floating in through the side windows of the dining room. Sounds on the Island have a unique and surprising way of being picked up on air currents and delivered, full bodied and pulsing, blocks away from their source.

We both knew, however, that this could only be coming from the nearby Navy yard gates at Caroline and Whitehead Streets. We rose quickly from the table and hurried to the front porch and down its steps to the lawn that was raised several feet above the sidewalk on Duval.

To our left, on the corner of Caroline and Duval a small crowd had gathered. In the other direction, two blocks up, another cluster of people could be seen in front of the dime store (now Fast Buck Freddy's). However, in the fresh morning sunlight, not a soul occupied the entire two blocks in between, except my grandfather and myself. We stood on our elevated perch waiting expectantly. Here came the Key West Chief of Motorcycle Police, Frank Caraballo, riding his big, black motorcycle proudly leading the Presidential departure, motors roaring, American flags flying from both handle bars. Next came members of the cabinet in limousines followed by several cars of Navy in white uniforms and waterfalls of gold braid. Finally, in an open touring car with Admirals Nimitz and Leahy, came the President waving and smiling, his eyeglasses glinting and flashing in the morning sunlight.

"Extraordinary," I thought as he slowly approached us, "how a man can seem to literally grow bigger physically with success!" Truman was smiling his big Roosevelt smile. "What a hard act that must be to follow," I thought., and I couldn't help admiring this cocky little man who now looked tanned and jubilant.

As the presidential car moved past the small crowd at the corner and headed up Duval with its empty morning sidewalks, the silence became deafening! Not a soul in sight for two blocks! Now almost abreast of us, we could see the President's raised arm, still waving, but begin to droop at the wrist, and on his face was a frozen anxious smile. Where was everybody? Where had they all disappeared ?

Then it happened! Pop, all five feet eight inches of him, stepped forward to the edge of his elevated front lawn. He stood for a moment, and then, in a splendid Shakespearean gesture as Truman sighted us, he stepped forward and bowed majestically. His right arm moved in a dramatic flourish out from his portly middle in a grand Sir Walter Raleigh bow and sweep, and in his best speaker's voice he boomed, "A PLEASANT VOYAGE TO YOU SIR! A PLEAS- ANT VOYAGE!!"

The response from the President was immediate and electric! Hidden batteries were suddenly and exquisitely recharged! Truman broke into an even wider grin, mouth opening, chin tilted up in pleasure as he waved and bowed in direct eye contact with my grandfather.

I will never forget this moment — the heady feeling of pride mixed with utter astonishment and enchantment at my grandfather's duplicity, and his generosity and gallantry!

But after all, this *was* Pop's Special Island, and passing by, on our Duval Street *was* the President of the United States!

President Truman arriving in Key West after his electon - entering the Presidential gates at Whitehead and Caroline.

Grace Dorgan Porter – c.1925

Livestock

My grandmother Grace Dorgan (Porter) was a beautiful blonde belle from Mobile, Alabama. In her social world she was considered a beauty not only by those who knew her, but also by those who knew of her. Grace, however, had a witty and realistic sense of humor, and told her spindly adolescent daughter later in life, to comfort her during this always difficult stage, "You don't have to be a beauty, Jessie, all you really need to do, is create the reputation for being a beauty."

Grace's family background was English, Scotch and Irish. Her maternal grandparents were the Scottish Ian Campbell, the youngest son of the Duke of Argyle, and his wife, Jean from Aberdeen, whom he had brought to the New World and for whom I was named. On Grace's Irish side, her father Lyle Dorgan, was a successful cotton and commodities broker with his base in New Orleans.

As was the custom in those days, businesses were in New Orleans, though the family homes of many successful businessmen were located in Mobile nearby; a shady river

The Dorgan family grown children

town and cultural hub that had not suffered too badly from the Civil War and had recouped rapidly afterward. Life was pleasant and gracious and hospitable in Mobile during the days before 1900. They were full of balls, teas and picnics on the river bluffs and lazy afternoons on porch swings.

The Dorgan family lived comfortably and securely with its four children. Grace was the oldest child with one sister and two younger brothers. It was a loving and close-knit family when their father Lyle suddenly and tragically died of a heart attack. Only after his death did the family discover the cause. It had been brought on by worry and overstrain due to a business crisis.

Lyle's older partner, whom he deeply respected and who had taken him into his business as a young man, came to him and confessed that he had made an ill-advised investment. Instead of accepting the losses, he had compounded them by throwing good money after bad. He had done this repeatedly over a period of time using first his

Mobile in 1880

own personal moneys, then the firm's. Now all was gone. They would be, he said, forced to declare bankruptcy. His younger partner was shocked but not paralyzed and proceeded to extricate and save both the business and his partner with his own personal finances. He did this in strict confidentiality, but the strain and worry of the effort weakened and finally destroyed his health. Within months after the beginning of this crisis, it brought on a fatal heart attack.

The family was distraught with grief but they rallied together in a loving fashion. Grace's mother knew of their economic plight, but confided only to her oldest daughter Grace that all that was left was their big house and a young family.

Grace Dorgan – 1890

All of Mobile came to Lyle Dorgan's funeral and its reception afterward. He had been a loved and popular business and social leader along with his attractive wife and lively family.

"What shall I tell them?" asked Grace's mother, Jessie, of her oldest child at the funeral reception. All of Lyle's business associates had come to his widow offering their services and help. It was assumed of course, that women were helpless with money matters and that Lyle had left his family well off.

"I can't tell them that father used up everything saving the business. That we have no money left."

In those days (1890s), the cattle business had become the most

Dorgan family visiting the Porters
in Key West – 1900

popular investment in the international world market. Many European investors, particularly wealthy English aristocrats, were turning with gusto to nature and the Wild West and investing in the cattle business. "What shall I say?" asked her mother with much uncertainty. "Just tell them," said Grace, eyeing in the distance all the younger Dorgan children in the living room, red eyed but comforting themselves with delicious funereal cakes. "Just tell them that Father left all his fortune in livestock."

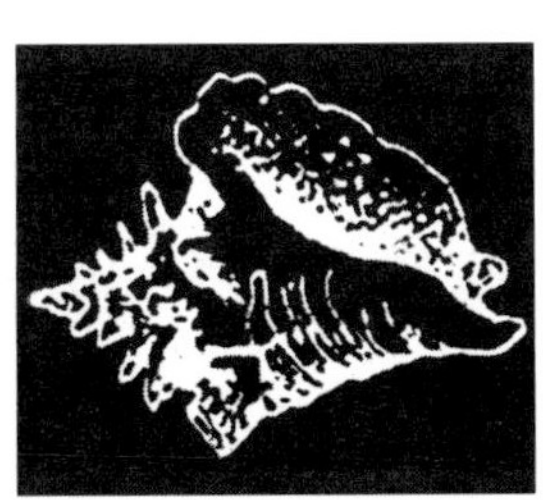

Family Wisdoms

* *This is happiness: Not what we see, but what we choose . . . . Not what we have, but what we use.*

— Jessie Dorgan

* *Before the age of fifty a man wants to show you what a MAN he can be – After the age of fifty, he wants to show you what a BOY he can be.*

— Big Mama, Grace Porter

* *Fashions rise and fall, come and go like the tides. Sooner or later we all get caught and beached with one. So make sure it's a becoming one to be stranded in.*

— Big Mama, Grace Porter

* *You don't have to be a beauty. All you need to do is create the reputation for being a beauty.*

— Big Mama, Grace Porter

Grace and Will Porter – 1939

Never give advice away unless it's paid for . . . otherwise it's never appreciated.

— Big Mama, Grace Porter

Rather a kind lie than a hurtful truth.

— Big Mama, Grace Porter

If you must do something that you don't really want to do but should do or have to do, do it with grace. Some unexpected bounty will always come from doing it that way.

— Big Mama, Grace Porter

Good manners get you further and cost you less than anything else in the world.

— Big Mama, Grace Porter

Pain hollows out the heart for joy.

— Big Mama, Grace Porter

Service is the rent you pay for being on the planet.

— Big Mama, Grace Porter

Willful waste makes woeful want.

— Jean from Aberdeen (Grace's grandmother, Jean Campbell)

*   *It's not the use, its the abuse (about liquor).*

> — Jean from Aberdeen

*   *Make the most of what you have
before you ask for anything more.*

> — Susan Brown Randolph

*   *If! If! If! If I had a drop of water in
Hell, I could sell it for a million dollars.*

> — Pop, W. R. Porter

*   *A sense of humor is a saving grace —
to spend lavishly.*

> — Miss Jessie

Grace Dorgan – 1900

*   *Written on the back of a family photo of three girls (Curry) that names
each one: "Alise Curry Newton, married in the Navy, husband became
Admiral John Henry Newton. Gladys Curry Boatwright, married in
the army, husband became General Boatwright. Louisa Curry, married
badly, died young."*

*   *We've set the day, but not the date.*

> — Pop's comment while stalling about
> getting married for the second time.

*   *An old Southern gentleman friend complained, "Young people today,
talk about anything. I mean ANYTHING — As a matter of fact, that's
ALL they DO talk about !"*

> — Miss Jessie

* *Miss Jessie — my mother — was a larger than life person with enormous energies . . . Energies in the plural because she had at least three extra auxiliary motors, one would kick in when the last had given out.*

— Jeane Porter

* *Like leaves on a tree, we all need to know when to let go.*

— Big Mama, Grace Porter

* *Do mystery writers usually write the ending first?*
"I know the answer. What is the question?" asked Gertrude Stein as she was dying in Paris. We all know the answers. We are programmed to know them, in genes and instincts, nerve reactions and hormones but what questions are we asking? This is what our civilization currently is failing, I think, to do.

— Jeane Porter

* *I always feel that children of famous and illustrious parents should be allowed and given a handicap, like golfers, in order to stay in the game and keep on playing . . . . They have a hard act to follow.*

— Jeane Porter

* *Courtesy is kindness in dress clothing.*

— Jessie Porter

* *History can be served up as a dry soda cracker or like a moist piece of chocolate cake. Which do you prefer?*

— Jessie Porter

* *Everybody is born in a box — a box of wealth or a box of poverty; a box of physical or mental limitation; a box of family problems or neglect. The fascinating thing to watch is to see how people manage to escape their boxes: some do it by clawing their way out, others by building ladders to climb out and others still by breaking down the walls to escape. A few, not many, simply stand up and walk out. But there are those who are content to remain in their boxes all their lives.*

— Big Mama, Grace Porter

* *There are those who don't know and there are those who don't know they don't know.*

— W.R Porter

* *A town or a city must know and preserve it's past so that it can understand its present and visualize its future.*

— Jeane Porter

Great Grandmother Jessie Dorgan

Heroes and heroines are the bright lights on our horizon by which we navigate by night.

— Jessie Porter

Robert Frost, Jessie (Porter Newton) and Kay Morrison on the 2nd floor porch of Heritage House - 410 Caroline in 1953

Family and Friends

Frost in the Garden
Out On A Limb
Sally Rand and her Fans
Tallulah
Jessie and Gloria
John Dewey
The View Was Marvelous
All in a Name
Reap the Wild Wind
Mardi Gras

Robert Frost by Alberto DeAndrea

Frost in the Garden

When I was a child, and later a teenager, and Robert Frost came to visit us here staying in the garden cottage, I never thought of him as a national or internationally famous poet, just as a pleasant older friend of my mother's. I remember that he said he enjoyed "Barding around" which I took to mean visiting friends. I think he had a small crush on Jessie; I know he enjoyed her and responded to her with enthusiasm. Once I heard them commiserating and agreeing with each other about how really basically shy each was and what effort it took to overcome this enormous handicap and how no one ever gave them credit for this bravery and heroic effort. I had to cover my mouth to keep from laughing, since both were such "on stage" people and they both loved the spotlight.

We all called him affectionately "Massa Robert," half in fun and half seriously since his full name was Robert E. Lee Frost. His mother had named him in honor of the confederate hero.

Patio and old Dutch Oven – Heritage House Gardens

"Massa Robert's" energy is still and even now present in the Heritage House garden where he enjoyed sitting and meeting friends in the afternoons. It is a strange but very pleasant feeling to hear his voice floating over to my cottage where I now live — freeing the big house to be a living house museum. His voice is, of course, taped and recites for visitors some of my favorite of his poems: *Swinger of Birches*, and *Mending Walls* and others.

The other night The Spectrelles, a trio of sequined bedecked cuties, were carolling full blast and had been for several hours from Kelly's Restaurant next door. They were perched on the newly constructed second floor open porch that now looks directly down the bosom cleavage of our old Heritage House gardens. By 11:45, I had had all I could take of this invasion and I stumbled out to the wet bar behind the old Dutch oven chimney, found the tape switch and turned on Robert Frost. His voice, deep, rather gravelly and very serious sounded out of the pitch black recesses of the garden just below where The Spectrelles were perched:

SOMETHING THERE IS THAT DOESN'T LIKE A WALL. It boomed sounding like God. THAT SENDS THE FROZEN GROUND SWELL UNDER IT. The poet's voice continued, trembling and vibrating the leaves with its volume, while the singing quavered and then went off key. GOOD FENCES MAKE GOOD NEIGHBORS . . . SPRING IS THE MISCHIEF IN ME. By now the singing had stopped dead, and then, like birds disarrayed by a hail of shot and brought down, tried to regroup and take flight again. The poet's voice continued at full blast. BEFORE I BUILT A WALL, I'D ASK TO KNOW WHAT I AM WALLING IN OR WALLING OUT. GOOD WALLS MAKE GOOD NEIGHBORS . . . by now putting the musical parakeets to full flight.

Minutes later their manager arrived. We discussed the possibilities of a battle of voices versus controlled volume. Needless to say, "Massa Robert" won this round — wings down.

Poet Robert Frost

John Dewey – Philosopher

Out on a Limb

"Man is thought in action."

- John Dewey

Mother and I first saw him standing under the Spanish cork tree shading the sidewalk on Telegraph Lane. It was a warm, pleasant, peaceful sunny morning — nothing untoward, amiss or seemingly threatening in nature anywhere in sight.

The older man was dressed in a clean but tattered white shirt with frayed sleeves and faded khaki trousers. He had a shock of gray-white hair that fell in a bang over his forehead and thin wired glasses perched on a weatherbeaten nose. We somehow knew he wasn't a bum or a snowbird, from some intangible message in his bearing, or perhaps it was the intense preoccupation and concentration he expressed bent over the sidewalk. As we approached, we saw that he was observing a long procession of brilliantly colored insects making its way across the cement sidewalk to the Spanish cork tree. The insects swarmed up the rough bark to disappear into the heart-shaped density of its leaves. As Mother and I came

42

abreast of him, he unbent and looked up and said in a rather rough gravelly voice, "Excuse me, do you know the name of these bugs?"

Jessie, surprised and pleased by the question, nodded.

"Yes," she said. "They are mostly Cochineal bugs, and they live on the Spanish cork tree."

"Cochineal. I have heard of them," he said. "Aren't they used for red dye by Indians in the Southwest?"

"And by Egyptian women in Pharaoh's court for lip rouge," said Jessie smiling.

We three turned to watch the procession again. The insects were fascinating, with a two-part body brilliantly scarlet in color, each part sharing one-half of a jet black diamond-shaped saddle. They looked like a marching Renaissance pageant in progress on parade, climbing up into the tree to disappear and then reappear again in a huge ball at the end of a high limb. As we watched, the ball twisted and writhed and suddenly the limb supporting it snapped! Down they came to the sidewalk in a scarlet, crimson

splash of color and a thousand bodies. John Dewey and the two of us looked down at the scene of carnage and survival in silence, and then the world famous philosopher commented wryly:

"Looks just like civilization to me," he said. "Gets itself out in a bunch at the end of a limb, overloads it, and then drops off!"

Jessie invited him over to the garden for drinks that afternoon. It was the beginning of a life-long friendship.

It was said that Dr. Dewey's wife prayed each night before she went to sleep; Oh Lord please take care of John. He can handle his enemies himself; but please, Lord, protect him from his friends.

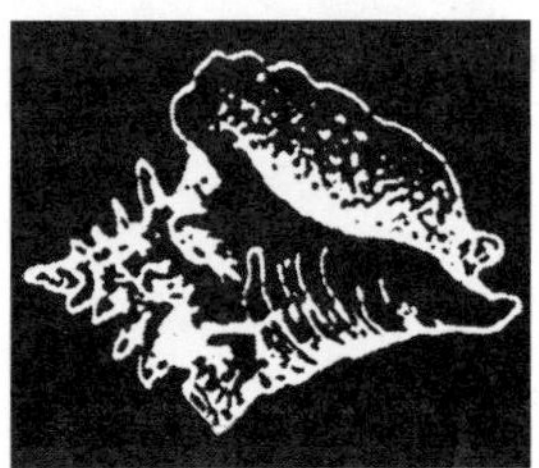

Sally Rand

Sally Rand and Her Fans

Were it not for her fans, Sally Rand would have been considered as great and as innovative a dancer as Isadora Duncan. Her plume fans, her "magic wands," were her undoing. Their "Now you see it, now you don't," Swan Lake elegance and tongue in cheek satire were too suggestive, too sexy to be considered a serious art form, and Sally was just too much fun, platinum blond pretty, to be taken seriously!

She would comment self-deprecatingly, "covering" herself in the company of such poetic notables and brainy academics as Robert Frost and John Dewey getting together in Miss Jessie's back garden at 410 Caroline Street, "I'm not very smart — I'm just a Missouri farm girl," and look with melting blue eyes at either man. One could visibly see their chest expansion in progress while Sally radiated sex appeal in all directions.

Everybody loved her, especially the Navy, from the lowest gob to the highest three stripe admiral. One of the Island's favorite gossip stories about her was her defense of an attractive young ensign who had spent such a late evening with her that he had overslept and missed

his ship's sailing at six the next morning.

When he was put in the brig Sally rushed over to plead his defense with the Admiral whom she also knew personally. "He's the best ensign in the entire U. S. Navy," she declared very emotionally to his superior officer.

Luckily the Admiral was an understanding and happily married man, so the young ensign wasn't court-martialed. He was just transferred rapidly to another duty station.

Sally's dance platform — her "Acropolis" — was the Havana Madrid Nightclub at the foot of Duval where Zero Duval stands today. It was an exotic, half-covered, half-open-aired patio nightclub featuring great town musicians, both Cuban and Conch orchestras, and Sally. Everybody loved to go there to dance and to see Sally perform with her enormous white plumed fans. She actually wore an entire body stocking, cream colored, not white and very deceptive because she had a beautiful lithe body that managed to look nude even when it wasn't.

Sally's only and occasional partner was an enormous, lazy and affectionate Python about eight feet long that she called Henry. One cool December morning she arrived at Jessie's door wringing her hands and terribly worried. Henry had disappeared.

"I don't know what to do," she lamented, tears in her eyes.

"He's so shy - people won't understand him. They could kill him."

Henry made his first appearance solo under the breakfast table in Sue Steinbrader's back garden. Her visiting aunt from Baltimore fainted dead away. His next appearance was a day later and a block away during an afternoon garden party at the Prince's. The whole gathering disbanded in all directions like autumn leaves in a high wind. Henry was finally found shaken and hiding out in the Otto's washhouse and Sally was notified. She came immediately and was terribly thankful and grateful.

"He has a slight cold," she told us, "from exposure, but other than that he's fine. Thank the Lord."

Henry was ready in a day or so to take to the stage again. He had learned that it was much safer there and with Sally than in the real world outside.

*   *   *

So on moonlit nights, when a jasmine scented breeze wafts over the Island and music is heard across the Strand, older Key Westers look up and see silvery palm fronds wave like plumes against fleecy white clouds floating across an indigo sky — and they remember Sally Rand.

Sally Rand's Havana Madrid night club. Jeane & Billy Spillman are doing the Tango. Celebration: Semaña Allegre Week. – 1942

Key West waterfront – Alice Bredon

The Haunting Tallulah

T allulah Bankhead was having tea by the fire at Heritage House. Playwright friends James Leo Herlihy and Tennessee Williams had brought the glamorous actress over to meet Miss Jessie. I had just returned home for a visit from Australia. Tallulah, leaning back languidly in a high winged-back armchair, was being a perfect Southern lady, right down to her long eyelashes and svelte suede pumps. Surprisingly, she was also a good listener. I had just told the gathering about visiting a wonderful old house the day before with Mother and the city manager in an effort to save it from destruction. The Caribbean classic (now the office of Knight's Realty on Duval) had recently been inherited by heirs who wanted to destroy it and erect a commercial building in its place with the excuse that it was in bad condition. It wasn't, and Miss Jessie persuaded the authorities to save it.

During the visit, I had picked up an old photograph on the floor, half hidden in a heap of debris. It was of a 1890s lady who

Tallulah Bankhead and Gary Cooper

looked like a female version of the laughing Cavalier, à la Franz Hals, she wore a black velvet plumed hat and a white lace collar over black silk. I had brought the photo home and put it on my desk to enjoy, knowing no one wanted or would miss it.

That evening, strange things had begun to occur in my great-grandfather's house where I was staying. Sudden drafts and cold rushes of air ran through the apartment and rapping sounds left me quite unnerved and mystified. I had a haunted feeling that an important message was trying to come through from the Laughing Lady in the photograph — but what?

Tallulah listened in rapt attention and then purred in her famous contralto: "My dear, I envy you so. I have always wanted to encounter a ghost . . . but as luck would have it . . . ." Her voice trailed off and we all leaned forward to urge her to continue.

"Well," she said, "it happened a few years ago when I was on tour and I dropped in to visit a cousin who owned a beautiful plantation outside of Lexington, Kentucky." The fire crackled on the hearth and Tallulah had us entranced.

"We had come down dressed for dinner and as I was having

my first martini — I underline first — when into the large entrance hall, perhaps a dozen yards away, walked an enormous white stallion. I saw it as plain as day — he was a magnificent beast!"

She stirred in the big comfortable wing chair. "Well, I turned toward my cousin Charles thinking surely he had seen it too, but he was sipping his drink and talking plantation talk with his friend, completely unaware. So I just finished my martini and had another — very quickly, I can tell you!

"The next evening at the same time the very same thing happened again! This time even before my first martini. I couldn't contain myself. 'Charles,' I said emphatically, trying to sound calm and matter of fact, 'I see a very large, beautiful white stallion standing in your entrance hall!'

"He wasn't a bit surprised, quite the contrary. He said, 'You do! You are so lucky! Other people have seen him too, but I've never been able to — dammit. That mount was Gallant Chief, the original sire of my entire blood-line of racing horses, many of whom have won the Derby! You are so lucky, Tallulah!'

"Lucky, well, I don't know about that," shrugged Tallulah laughing. "Here I have always wanted to see a ghost, but wouldn't you know it would be that of a horse!"

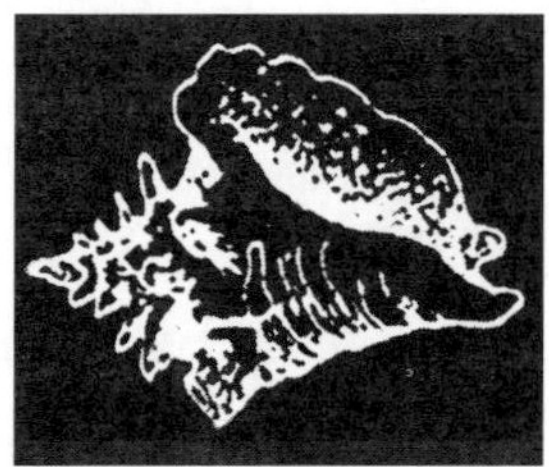

Gene Otto, Mitchell Wolfson, Gloria Swanson and her latest protegé in
The Heritage House's Garden - Jessie took this picture. c.1965

Jessie and Gloria

Miss Jessie should have gone on the stage like her girl-hood playmate and friend, Gloria Swanson, but in her day "nice girls" didn't do that wild and immoral thing unless they were (society was sure) just that: wild and immoral.

Gloria started out at age twelve on the stage of the old Odd Fellows' Hall (or Garden Theatre) on Caroline Street next door to Heritage House here in Key West. She had a deep, contralto voice and a sultry delivery even at that tender age, and no mother to say "No! You can't." — so she did and became famous, had countless husbands and never lost her looks, thanks partly to her belief in health foods and yoga exercise, and to her lovely high cheek bones.

One afternoon in the late 40s, Mother and I were puttering in the Heritage House back garden when down the side driveway in from Caroline Street came three figures: two very tall men, one blond and athletic looking, the other older and balding, a bit rotund in the mid-dle, both attractive. Between them a svelte, beautiful little woman made even more diminutive by the height of her two companions. She was as exquisite as a Greek Tenegran figurine with dark chestnut hair styled in a page-boy, high arched eyebrows and winged gray-green eyes. As she approached us, her face brightened and she said in a low, musical voice, "Excuse me, can you help us? I'm looking for Jessie Porter."

Jessie, in a gardening outfit — what were they called? — large coveralls with legs widened at the bottom — culottes — felt instantly rustic and unkempt by comparison, nevertheless, responded politely, "I'm Jessie Kirke now. I was Jessie Porter."

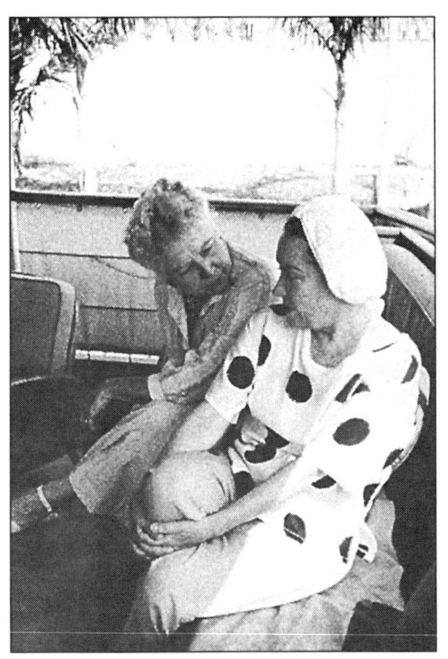

Gloria Swanson and Jessie on Gloria's yacht.

The woman's face brightened ever further into a radiant smile.

"Jessie," she exclaimed, arms wide, "don't you recognize me? I'm Gloria!"

It was the triumphant return of the almost native to her childhood playground. Gloria's father had been stationed here in the army before World War I. When her mother had died he had come to Jessie's mother and asked, "When you dress Jessie, would you dress Gloria too? I don't know much about these things."

Grace Porter had, of course, agreed with pleasure. Gloria was an attractive and appealing child and Grace had a wonderful dressmaker named Empira who sewed beautifully for the whole family.

Gloria had left Key West in her early teens, having made her debut at the Odd Fellows Hall and had, it seemed, almost instantly catapulted into fame as a femme fatale movie star. She had an individual and unique comic twist all her own, becoming one of the greatest vamps of the Silver Screen. Several lives and many husbands later, here she was back in Key West again.

Her companions were Sarner, the famous music publisher, and the other, her latest protégé: a young Swedish photographer whom she was helping to launch professionally. She had done this in the past with many budding talents including, surprisingly, Desi Arnaz. Now Gloria and her friends had arrived here on Gloria's luxurious rented yacht that was berthed nearby in the Navy yard and that was manned by a handsome captain and a selectively attractive all-male crew, in true "Gloria" style.

Gloria was still coming up roses. She was an excellent businesswoman and had made and saved a lot of money thanks partially to the backing of Joe Kennedy Sr., with whom she had had a child, a son. And though she later grew to resent and dislike him intensely, she kept their secret and his reputation well guarded until after his death, and beyond.

Mother and Gloria kept in touch and saw each other in Key West or in New York often after this. Gloria owned a castle in Portugal and invited Jessie and her husband, Newt, to visit her there, but they were never able to.

In my salad days in the early 50s, when I was studying painting in Europe, I was in a movie with Gloria's daughter Michelle, in Monte Carlo. It was filmed in the Summer Casino with Michelle playing the lead. They filmed two simultaneous versions, a French and an English one, and Michelle had two leading men, one for each version. By the end of each day she was in exhausted tears.

Though she looked much like her mother and was just as beautiful, it was stressful work. She ended up marrying her producer and living in Paris. Probably the title of her first and only film, and mine, had a lot to do with her choice of life styles! The film was called Monte Carlo Baby. As a cinema actress, however, her mother Gloria was made of more enduring stuff, and her image will shine on the silver screen forever.

Gloria's message to me when I was a teenager as we sat in the garden talking one day was, "Never say you can't or won't do something, because inevitably that is what life always makes us do."

"The Everglades" houseboat owned by Colonel Robert Thompson. My parents spent their honeymoon on this boat.

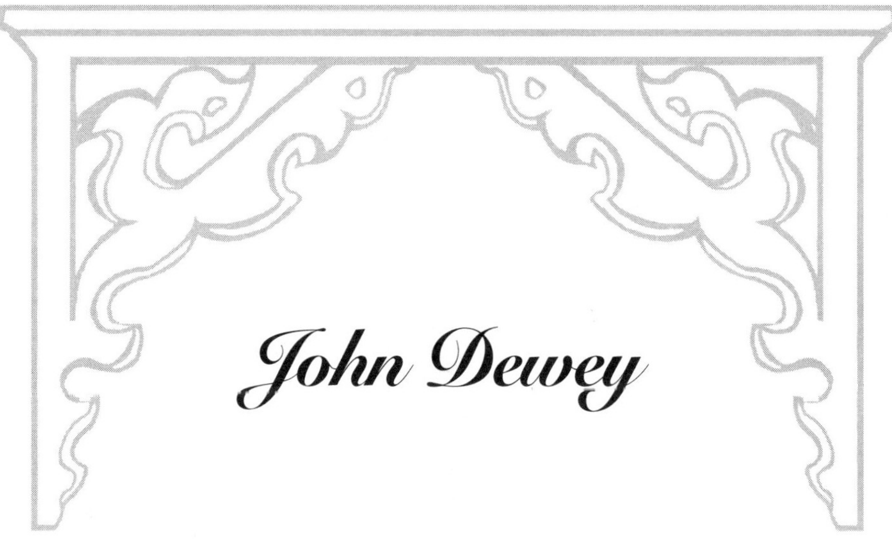

John Dewey

"Thought is man in action." – John Dewey

In the 1930s and 40s John Dewey had become a leading world philosopher as well as an American icon. His ideas and concepts are so interwoven into contemporary education, that his "learn by doing" processes are synonymous with teaching practices today and have become inseparable. In the 30s and 40s, however, it was all "revolutionary" and "modern," an important departure from the staid and academic world of book and rote learning.

In the spring of 1938 the Bentleys, Irma, Cal and their two teenage girls, came sailing (steaming) down to Key West on their beautiful 170 foot yacht "The Susquehanna" and anchored in the Navy yard at the foot of Caroline Street. Irma, who had met my mother several winters before, hurried over to find her friend again at 410.

"Oh, Jessie" she said earnestly, "I've been tutoring the girls while we were at sea and using John Dewey's ideas for inspiration and guidelines."

Left to right; John Dewey, Max Eastman, Alexander Barmine seated on the porch of one of the cabañas on Rest beach.

Irma was an attractive, neat and intensely earnest woman who was doing her best, while married to a successful industrialist and millionaire, not to lose her common touch.

She continued: "Jessie, I've read everything — EVERYTHING — John Dewey has ever written, and I can honestly say that his writing has changed my entire life!" She paused, looking intently into Jessie's face, "I know he's a neighbor and a friend of yours."

She continued hesitantly, "Could you — do you think you could arrange for me to meet him? It would mean so much to me!"

Jessie, seeing how important this was to her friend, agreed that of course she would arrange it, and as soon as possible.

Dr. John, as we called him, lived then just down Telegraph Lane on nearby Greene Street with his two daughters, Jane and Evelyn. He much enjoyed being invited to Jessie's garden for afternoon get-togethers, relishing the mixed and interesting assortment of people Jessie always collected there. Fan dancer Sally Rand was one of his favorites, along with poet Robert Frost, playwright Thornton Wilder and others.

That afternoon, writer Bob Thielen and his wife Helen were having a cocktail party. Jessie found Dr. Dewey at the gathering happily imbibing his third martini.

"Dr. John," she began after they had greeted each other, "I've a friend who has just arrived here on her yacht that is anchored nearby in the Navy yard. She says she has read everything you have ever written and she wants so much to meet you. She says that what you have written has changed her whole entire life!"

Dr. Dewey looked down at the attractive, animated Jessie with deep curiosity and affection. "That so?" he rumbled. "What did I say?"

"I'm not sure," Jessie answered undaunted, "but she says it has changed her entire life!"

"Maybe so," responded the world's leading philosopher, "but it didn't get me a yacht!"

*   *   *

"The only thing that doesn't change is the essence of change itself." — John Dewey

*   *   *

When the battling heirs of the Oldest House (Wrecker's Museum) finally put it up for sale, (Miss Mae Douglas had left it to 73 heirs, sometimes three to a room.) Miss Jessie deposited $2,000 to hold the house and contacted Marion Bentley Wall (daughter of Irma and Cal), urging her to buy it. Generously Marion did this, restored it, and gave it to the Old Island Restoration Foundation and the City.

Richard Halliburton on Elizabeth the elephant going over the Alps

The View Was Marvelous

Richard Halliburton

In the financially strapped period before World War II when America was still recuperating from the Great Depression, Richard Halliburton became a national alter ego and our favorite escape artist. He did everything everyone had ever dreamt of doing, and what the most adventurous didn't have the money to do, and then some: He swam the Hellispont like Hercules; leapt into the Sacred Well at Chichen Itza and survived; swam the Suez Canal as the S. S. Halliburton and, yes, went over the Alps like Hannibal on an elephant. When last heard from he was sailing out into the China Seas in a junk, and according to final reports was caught in a typhoon. Sadly, he was never heard from again. It was probably the way Richard would have chosen to go out of this world — on a wave of high adventure.

He was an unusually attractive and a very blond young man full of energy and excitement. Jessie had invited him to the garden for lunch along with Gene and Anne Otto. Gene was Key West's most talented and leading native artist and Anne his beautiful bride. They had met in Paris where Gene had captured and married her and recently brought her back to Key West. They and several other

Ft. Jefferson and Bush Key

guests, including Richard Halliburton were enjoying a languid lunch at Miss Jessie's at 410 together.

Dick had center stage. He was young, in his thirties, a transient journalist on assignment to write a story about Dr. Mudd and Fort Jefferson at Dry Tortugas for the *Saturday Evening Post*. His article would feature Dr. Mudd as an American "Dreyfus" and Fort Jefferson as America's "Devil's Island." It would make a fascinating story, he was certain, and Miss Jessie and her guests all agreed.

"But," continued the young man, "what I'd really like to do next after this assignment is to go over the Alps like Hannibal." Here he paused and looked around the table. "But where in the world will I ever find an elephant?"

"That's an easy one to answer," said Gene laughing, "I know just where and how!"

We all turned to listen, knowing that history in the making was not a new happening in Key West. Gene proceeded, "I used to paint often," he said, "near the zoo in the Paris Bois des Vincennes. There I became friends with the old elephant keeper, Emile. He personally owns an ex-circus elephant named Elizabeth that he keeps there. But Emile wants to retire. I bet you could buy her for a song if you promised to love and cherish her and furnish her with a ton of hay a day."

Richard was pleased with the suggestion and wrote the keeper's name in his notebook for future reference. The next day he arranged to have a boat take him to the Dry Tortugas and Fort Jefferson. Several months later we read his article in the *Saturday Evening Post*. It was most interesting.

A few months passed and the memory of that luncheon had faded when an envelope postmarked from a small town in the Swiss Alps arrived in Miss Jessie's mail. It contained a photo of our hero astride a large and happy looking elephant surrounded by crowds of admiring children. In the background were the snow-crested Alps.

The message read: "The view of the Alps is wonderful - especially from the back of an elephant! Many thanks for the special lunch that made this adventure possible." It was signed Dick and Elizabeth.

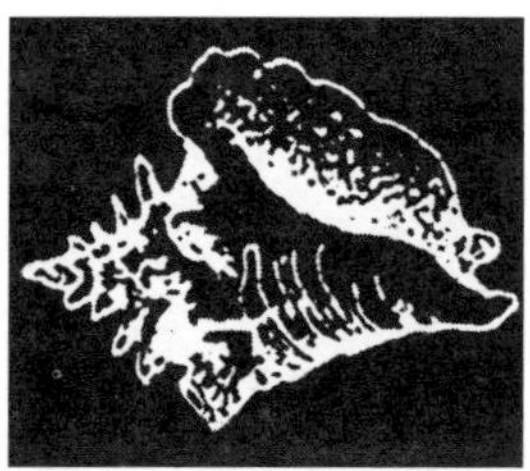

Bahama Village Key West, by William Cantwell

All in a Name

But John," said Miss Jessie, comforting her friend. "Your book is wonderful!" John Erskine, professor of history at Columbia University, had just arrived for a visit to escape the bleak winter weather of New York City. In spite of the balmy Key West climate, he was feeling very low in spirit, since the book he had researched and labored on for well over a year had almost been ignored by the critics and the reviewers with its recent publication.

He couldn't understand why. It was about one of the world's most fascinating women, Helen of Troy: La Belle Hélène, as she has been known by history ever since.

Some years after the Trojan War had ended, Telemachus, looking for his father Ulysses, arrived at the Castle of Menelaus, King of Sparta. The King, remembering and admiring Telemachus' father, invited the young man for dinner. Ten years had passed since the war had ended and everyone had returned home except Ulysses. The Homeric story goes that while Telemachus and Menelaus (Helen's cuckold husband), along with other male guests, dined in macho "for men only" fashion, in walked the ravishing Helen as if nothing had happened. It was as if time had spun backwards . . . and that she had never turned the whole Aegean world upside down . . . as if the greatest Armada in ancient history had never been launched to recapture her from Paris and bring her back from Troy. Here she was as unruffled and beautiful and charming as ever, and very much at home.

The young Telemachus was immediately enchanted by her, but surprised by her manner. Her husband was completely recaptivated and she was obviously back ruling the roost as Queen of the realm once again. How did she manage to accomplish this? John Erskine, a professor of Classics at Columbia, was intrigued as well, and so he wrote a book about it.

"It's almost a complete no sale, "he lamented to Jessie. "It's sitting like a dead duck in the water about to sink."

Miss Jessie had read his book that he had given her a few days earlier. She had enjoyed it so much that she couldn't put it down.

"John, it's a fascinating book!" she exclaimed. "It's beautifully written and has an enthralling story line." She paused, thinking. "There's no reason in the world why it shouldn't sell — except maybe — the title is wrong."

Erskine, as an academician and a teacher, had called the book something that reflected his scholarly background.

"Why don't you give it another title — something less academic and more exciting?" asked Miss Jessie. "Something as appealing as Helen herself was? She was an enchantress. She certainly comes through as that in your book. Why not call it something more alluring like, "The Private Life of Helen of Troy?"

Erskine whistled outloud and agreed. He called his editor that afternoon. The book was recalled and retitled, and became a runaway best seller.

Reap the Wild Wind
Thelma Strabel

Key West owes a debt of warm gratitude to the writer Thelma Strabel. We should not forget how her book, Reap the Wild Wind (1941), a tale set in Key West at the height of the wrecking days (1850-60), helped to put Key West back on the visitors' map. It was a success, both as a book and then as a movie — an extravaganza directed by the master of extravaganza, Cecil B. DeMille. DeMille, as was his usual habit, took much of the credit for everything: the story, the characters, a Hollywood storm shot under and above water, and, yes, even Key West's colorful history. But it was a delightful film, and still is. It has first-class cinematic magic and effects that include vapory mists that must have been floated down on film from New England — since we rarely ever have them here. The giant squid in the film was the great-grandfather of multitudes of mechanical movie monsters to follow. Many of the film's characters existed in reality: Maritime Court Judge Marvin, and the villain, John Houseman, played by Raymond

Massey with wonderful Massey sneers and doleful hostile glances. Ray Milland was the elegant sea lawyer/hero and Paulette Goddard was young, spunky and beautiful. It was John Wayne's first part in big-time film, and the only one where he didn't get the girl.

The film's production company came to Key West in preparation for the filming, taking photos all over Old Town. Both Heritage House and the Tradewinds (the Caroline Lowe House on Caroline and Duval Streets) were photographed in detail and later combined and recreated in Hollywood to become the home of Loxi, the heroine.

Thelma Strabel

Thelma, a friend of my mother's, was a most attractive and very bright woman who had done extensive research into Key West history as background for her book. She was a much traveled, creative and talented person who knew many world-famous people, including Frank Lloyd Wright. I remember her telling this story about Wright.

He had been visiting with her (as her lover?) at her New York apartment when the doorbell rang in the middle of the night. It was after 2:30 a.m. Wright got up, very disgruntled, and opened the door. Standing there was an excited young newspaper man from the *New York Times*. "Sir," he said, once he had been told gruffly that he was talking to the famous architect, "We've just received a cable from Japan. There has been a terrible earthquake there and Tokyo is in total shambles. Have you anything to say to the press about your Imperial Hotel?"

"Tell the world," growled Wright, much annoyed at being awakened at that hour, "that the Imperial Hotel is still standing!" and slammed the door. According to Thelma, he never doubted for a moment that its floating foundation and earthquake-resistant capabilities had prevailed, and he was right: All of Tokyo looked like broken matchboxes, but his creation, the beautiful Imperial Hotel, was still standing and intact.

Thelma bought a part of the southernmost property at the end of Whitehead and South Streets from my great aunt and uncle, the Harrises, in the early 1940s. She built a charming, small, informal, open-to-sea-air cottage to settle into with the money she made from her book. Since then, the house has gone through several transformations until it now resembles a marbelized Venetian Palazzo.

I hope Thelma's spirit is somewhere around or visits us still. She managed to catch the spirit and heart of Key West's exciting wrecking days more than any other writer I know.

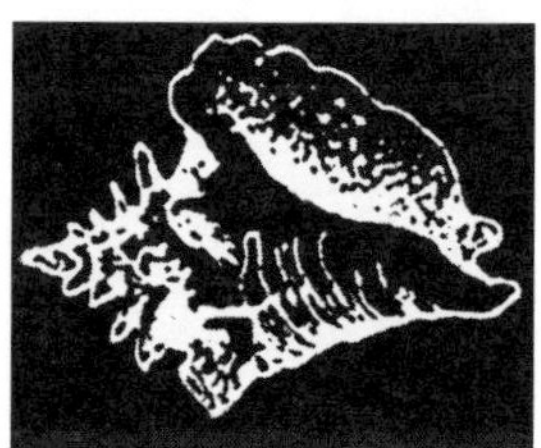

Grandfather Dakin and Tennessee at home

Mardi Gras

I 'm already two days late," lamented the older gentleman beside me, Tennessee Williams' beloved Grandfather Reverend Dakin. He was dressed in his usual severe ministerial garb and high white clergyman's collar. We were sitting, he ram rod straight side by side at the bar of the Rainbow Room in the La Concha Hotel. In the background a festive birthday party for writer James Leo Herlihy was in full swing. Listening to Grandfather Dakin, who was such a dignified Southern gentleman, I thought surely he must be speaking about an important medical appointment or church affair that he was missing.

"That boy" he said both lovingly and accusingly — "Tom — PROMISED he'd take me." he continued, referring to his grandson, Tennessee. "He said we'd go several days ago, but we keep getting sidetracked and held up by friends and parties like this." He paused and then continued emotionally: "If we don't get going and leave here soon," he said, "I'm going to miss the *whole entire Mardi Gras!*"

I remember new acquaintances, upon seeing that Grandfather

Dakin was a minister, would make polite conversation by asking him what branch of the Episcopal Church did he represent? "Well," he would respond with a glint in his eye, "High Church is crazy. Middle Church is hazy, and Low Church is lazy, and I'm High Church!"

*　　*　　*

Miss Jessie once asked Tennessee why he didn't use his grandfather as literary inspiration, instead of depressed people such as Mrs. Stone, one of his heroines. "He's such a positive lover of life," she said. To which Tennessee replied, "No drama there, Jessie."

*　　*　　*

Tennessee used to bring his mother over when she was visiting him here and would occasionally deposit her at my mother's for lunch. She was quite a beautiful, very Southern, older woman who wore big sun-stopping hats draped with white gossamer veils, rather like Blanche DuBois. She went around, I thought, disguised like an elegant beekeeper. (of course she was the prototype for the mother in Glass Menagerie)

After finishing one lunch, my Mother signaled to me, couldn't I take Mrs. Williams off her busy hands and somewhere with me? So I invited her to ride out to pick up my three children at the beach. She was delighted to come. As we were driving along talking casually about different things, she said regretfully how sorry she was that she had never had any grandchildren. Then she added, "But I suppose Tom's plays could be considered my grandchildren." She paused reflecting, and then commented wryly, "However, some of them could be considered rather naughty."

Tennessee used to say that many old Key West families had eccentric members. Considering his own, that was like the prover-

Frank Merlo, Tennesse Williams & Grandfather Dakin enjoying Havana

bial pot calling the kettle black.

I am most grateful to Tennessee for speaking so beautifully at my mother's memorial service, and to him as a friend. Tennessee had a very kind and compassionate heart. Cruel and insensitive criticism was a major factor in destroying him. It is fortunate that his grandfather died before his downward spiral began. I think he would have lived longer and produced even greater work had he been allowed to go through the experimental changes that are inevitable and necessary in the development of a great artist had he received more tolerance and less destructive criticism. I remember one prominent critic describing him and his place in the American theater as a "black hole" into which he and his talent has disappeared.

The island was most fortunate to have had him in residence for so many years. We miss him greatly!

"Go to sea in your car," WPA poster advertising
the new Overseas Highway.

Hemingway

I Remember Papa
The Hemingway Boys
Pauline's Easter Egg hunt
When the Sunsets and the
Bells Toll

Jeane, Patrick and Bumby Hemingway playing pirates in the Hemingway garden.

I Remember Papa

I don't believe Ernest Hemingway was called "Papa" by the world until after World War II. His sons John (Bumby), Patrick and Gregory of course called him Papa. As a child, I always felt he was a great father and very good to all of us children.

I remember his laughing and saying about his sons, "Three boys are just right! One to bait the hook! One to throw the line overboard. One to pull in the fish."

Mother commented to a friend when she first met Hemingway, "He looks like he breathes more air than most people." I think she was very aware of his attractive masculinity.

Playing in the Hemingway gardens during the 30s and 40s, we children all had to observe one firm rule, and that was: not to disturb Papa before noon by making any noise playing in the garden while he was writing above the pool house. Promptly at twelve he would descend the circular wrought iron stairs from his lair to join the world. I remember his coming down one noon, looking disheveled, muttering to himself and to anyone who could hear

The Hemingway house before the pool and wall were added.

him, in this case, me. "I've just written one sentence seventy-eight different ways!" I remember feeling sorry for him.

Visitors to the Hemingway House today should be reminded what a great word stylist he was, not just an icon. I can clearly remember when the world was full of young men in trench coats trying to look world weary and talking in truncated sentences à la-Hemingway. Everybody tried to emulate him — and many still do.

The Hemingway garden had peacocks in those days, strutting around majestically until we children pursued them, trying to catch them and pluck a tail feather. Fortunately, we didn't succeed often. There were six-toed cats in the neighborhood that would wander freely across the terrain of the garden, and the boys had raccoons in cages all named after their favorite movie stars. These included Greta Garbo, Harold Lloyd, Buster Keaton, Charlie Chaplin and Marlene Dietrich among others. One morning when we looked into the cages to play with them, we found that Greta Garbo had not only killed Harold Lloyd, but was busily eating him.

Patrick, then about eight years old and already a budding naturalist even at that early age, warned everybody: "Don't put your hands in the cage — she could be rabid." We all stood back and had to wait impatiently until noon for Papa to descend to the garden and then rushed in a clutch over to him, excitedly describing the tragedy in progress.

Papa went over and took a look and then turned to Bumby, the eldest of us, and said, "Go get the Remington.... shotgun!" Hemingway had a large collection of hunting arms of every description in cabinets and on certain walls within the house. The guns all had names and serial numbers which he used to identify them.

In minutes, Bumby returned with a small shot gun and handed it to his father. Within the cage Greta Garbo raised her moist snout toward us, gazing at us with shiny, black shoe-button eyes and holding up bloody paws. Hemingway opened the cage door and pointed the gun nozzle several inches from her forehead. There was a loud explosion and Greta Garbo's head disintegrated into the universe.

We kids were in shock for several days afterwards.

I remember sitting with the boys on the perimeter of the adult conversations where we were generally forgotten. In spite of being one of the best word stylists in the business, Hemingway had two favorite adjectives that he used often in conversation: "Swell" and "lousy."

In discussing writing and writers, which they did extensively, the conversation would sometimes gravitate to someone asking, "How is so-and-so in bed?" Hemingway's response was always characteristically brief: "Swell" or "lousy," he would respond if he qualified. It always left us children puzzled.

Another short glimpse of Hemingway; he said he always woke up at dawn because his eyelids were so thin that the light woke him so he would get up and write.

I asked Pauline once; did she ever consider marrying again? She shook her head, looking wistful and said, "No - I don't think so. I doubt if I will ever find another man like Ernest."

Hemingway's boat the Pilar was tied here at Craig Docks, now called Key West bight.

The Hemingway Boys

Patrick was the scientist of our expeditions. He was very smart; always collecting insects. "Isn't this a fascinating specimen" he would ask in wonder, while delicately holding up a Key West bug wiggling in his fingers.

Bumby, the Pirate Chief (in the photo on pg. 76) was a bit older (2-3 years) than the rest of us and of course, the leader in all our makeup games.

He was such a beautiful looking boy, more than just handsome, blonde and blue eyed with high color and dramatic energy and charm. Everything came so easily, effortlessly to him or so it seemed. Perhaps too easily for his own good. He spoke French and Spanish fluently by the time he was seven or eight. His father having taking him back to Paris and Spain where he picked up the languages almost by osmosis.

One winter, Sidney Franklin, the American bullfighter from Brooklyn, came to visit the Hemingways in Key West and brought Bumby a beautiful bullfighter's costume. I can still see Bumby flourishing his cape and sword dramatically with his brothers playing the charging bulls, lucky that no one lost an eye. The matador costume, a gift from Pauline, is on view in Heritage House.

As Flash Gordon and Dale, Bumby and I used to `shoot for the moon` stradling the cannons on the ramparts of Ft. Taylor; or recast ourselves as Tarzan and Jane in my tree house in 410's back garden. He was an exciting playmate and my first crush. I thought he was wonderful.

Pat and I saw each other a number of times later on as grown ups when he was in Stanford and I was going to Berkeley and later back here in Key West after he married Hennie, a lovely girl from Baltimore and brought her here to visit. I remember his wit and humor with delight and pleasure.

I always think that children of famous and illustrious parents should be allowed handicaps like golfers so that they can stay in the game and keep on playing. They have a very hard act to follow.

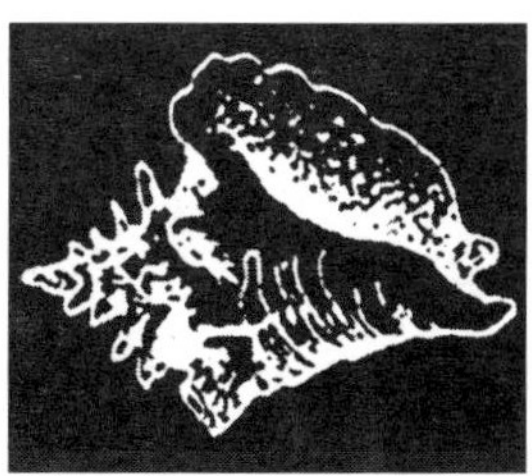

Pauline's Easter Egg Hunt

S ome of the prettiest memories of my childhood come with Pauline Hemingway's Easter Egg Hunts and luncheons held in the gardens of their house on Whitehead Street. I don't remember "Papa" being around, he was probably out fishing. But his friend and "Man Friday," Toby Bruce, was often there, standing by. Pauline and the nurse the three boys had almost outgrown, Aida, must have spent hours and days beforehand dying eggs and then hiding them all over the gardens on the pool side of the house. They were secreted along both walls of the property, in crests of low palms, in the crooks of plants, under leaves, half hidden in ingenious and unexpected places that were always surprising and fun. Years later I tried to emulate the magic of these hunts for my own children. But they were never as wonderful, I'm sure, as Pauline's.

About fifteen to twenty children, as I remember, were invited each year to come after church on Easter Sunday. It became an Island ritual. First the hunt, and afterward, a lovely lunch served at a long table on the side porch.

Pauline was a diminutive little gamin of a woman, sometimes with a dark cap of close-cropped black hair with peaked sideburns.

It has been said that the flapper of post-World War I hit two stylish birds with the same well-aimed stone: the French prostitute, with dramatically made-up eyes, cheeks and lip rouge, and the "pretty boy," in the trenches, flat chested, no hips and with boyish bobbed hair. Pauline related to these styles, but had her own individual and androgynous version that Ernest very much liked in his women. Maria in *For Whom the Bell Tolls*, for example, had short-cropped hair and wore men's clothes.

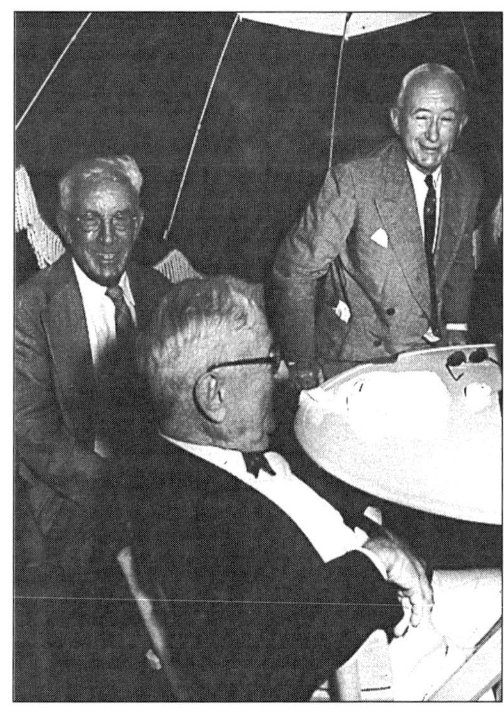

Meeting of the Highway Commission (J.B. Sullivan at left W.R. Porter in foreground.)

Photographs of Pauline don't do her justice, and never flatter her. She was unusually attractive and appealing, with a kind of chiseled, delicate beauty. She was a boy's mother, not a girl's mother. Perhaps that was one of the reason's I especially liked her, since I was a tomboy and enjoyed doing more what boys liked doing: climbing trees, building tree houses, swimming (especially underwater), foot racing, fishing, and sailing. The Hemingway boys and I all collected menageries: raccoons, chameleons and other lizards, stray dogs and cats, birds escaping hawks and traps, turtles, crickets, and occasionally snails. I remember traveling in the car with a large land snail that happily ate sandwich lettuce all the way from New York to Florida. One night en route, I left the net off the top of its jar in a tourist cabin where we had stopped for the night. When I woke the next morning, there was a long shiny ribbon trail going up the wall, behind the bed. It traversed the entire ceiling and descended the other side to the bathroom and to the tub where it had halted and camped on the moist grilled drain. Thirsty! We are probably living today with the descendants of that energetic, determined and prolific snail in the Heritage House gardens!

The Easter Egg Hunt parties were very, very special and such a pretty sight to see: Children all dressed in their Easter finery coming straight from church, running and darting back and forth across the lush, tropical gardens. Stooping, picking up eggs, shouting with delight and pleasure. The quota, I believe, was twelve eggs per child as a limit.

One particular Easter, when I was ten or eleven, I had been dressed to the hilt by my grandmother, who adored clothes and dressing me. To this day I feel uncomfortable at having to be more than casually dressed. Clothes always had to be guarded, taken care of and protected, and they always got in the way of "real" fun.

On this day I was wearing an imported white Swiss dress with tiny emerald green dots, from Altman's that was beautifully smocked in it's front and sleeves. Under it I had on new silk panties with rosebuds and white silk socks with green leaves and more rosebuds, and brand new, very white and shiny patent leather shoes, whose straps had mother-of-pearl buttons. All this starched and standing-out finery was supported underneath by a chambray petticoat trimmed with eyelet lace, and the total affair topped off by an enormous, monumental mint green and white striped hair ribbon. The bow was clasped securely by a silver barrette to my very straight black hair (that my grandmother, trying to make humor out of a liability, called "Chinese curls") that was bobbed to show the tips of my earlobes in Dutch-boy style. I was really a sight!

I had played in the gardens so often that I knew all the hiding places, and it had taken me only minutes to fill my egg quota. Now I was waiting for the others to finish the hunt, teetering in my new slippery-soled patent leather shoes along the edge of the pool. Of course, I was not only tempting fate, but going out to meet it.

Sully (J.B. Sullivan, a Hemingway favorite), the crusty and benevolent father of three of my friends, Letty, Teresa and Mary Sullivan, was lounging on the patio of the pool house having a drink and watching the hunt with abstracted pleasure. His amused, discerning Irish eyes caught sight of and recognized my 'game' immediately, so that when the inevitable happened — and I fell into the pool up to my chin — he was well prepared and knew just what to say: "Feels just like a bad dream, doesn't it," he said compassionately.

I shall always be grateful, and will never forget this unexpected and unprecedented sympathy and compassion coming from, of all people, an adult, as I stood there paralyzed in the brackish pool water in my ruined finery. The only thing that had stayed dry at all was the enormous hair bow!

Moments later Pauline saw and, laughing, rescued me from this calamity and ushered me into the pool-house bathroom, where I changed into my dry bathing suit. At lunch, with us children all sitting together at a long table, everyone else was showing off their Easter outfits. Even the boys in their white linen jackets, white shirts, bow ties and starched white shorts, now somewhat grass-stained, even they looked unaccustomedly elegant and were enjoying it, while I sat there in my one piece bathing suit, feeling naked.

Never mind, it was wonderful fun — a real treat, and such a lovely memory!

Thank you again, Pauline!

When the Sun Sets and the Conch Train Rolls

The reedy Southern voice reverberated and ricocheted along Whitehead Street from the Conch Train loudspeaker. "And now, folks, we are approachin' the home of the famous writer Ernest Hemingway, on your left. He lived for twelve years here. See that brick wall?" the driver paused and pointed. "His wife Pauline had that put up to corral him in, but he jumped it anyhow and headed straight for Sloppy Joe's Bar on Duval Street. Sloppy's was where he met his third wife, Martha Gelhorn," the guide continued as though he had been present. "Martha picked him up and packed him off to Cuba. It was curtains for Pauline!" He continued knowingly, "Hemingway did some of his best writin' while he lived here on the Island — but most of it was purely frictional!"

My family and I used to climb aboard the Conch Train each time we returned home from abroad. It was an Island homecoming ritual and a delight. When the drivers, mostly young men from Tennessee, were allowed to add their own creative flourishes

Commodore David Porter 1780-1843

to an already fascinating tapestry of local history, their tour descriptions could often be very hilarious and unexpected.

"Remember what I told you about Commodore David Porter?" asked one driver as the train rounded the corner of Caroline and Duval. "Well, he must have been some tough old bird, 'cause he's got relatives down here to this day. In fact," he paused and pointed in my direction as I stood in spattered work clothes mesmerized, and caught in the act of painting the Porter House corner wrought iron gate. Forty Ohioans in flowering sport shirts, straw hats and sunglasses all turned to stare, dark moon-eyed in my direction. "In fact," the guide repeated, voice rising triumphantly, finger pointing directly at me, "there's an ancestress there, RIGHT NOW!"

As I closed my mouth, I reflected sagely that it was good to know that you didn't have to die to become an 'ancestress'. All you had to do was just wait for the Conch Train to pass by.

Conch Train and Station at the Aquarium

William Randolph Porter – 1898
Courting Grace

Pop William Randolph Porter

Ah, Youth
In Deep
Still Open Sesame
All Aboard
Big Guns
Smoking
Perspective

*Dr. Joseph Y. Porter House built 1838. Duval & Caroline Streets.
The Montsart roof and balconies were added in 1898 by
Grandmother Louisa Porter who loved to "guild the lilly."*

Ah, Youth

In his youth, Pop (W.R. Porter) was very much a bounder. He was a man's man but he also enjoyed women and they him, and he treated them with much gallantry.

As a small boy, his high spirits and energy often got him into trouble with `the powers that be.' To calm him down and chastise him his mother would send him to bed during the day to consider his transgressions. He always wore a knee length white cotton night shirt and did so all his life.

The story goes that the town was celebrating President (General) Grant's visit here on his around the world tour with a big parade and marching bands high stepping it down Duval Street. The parade would end at the Jefferson Hotel with a bedecked and garlanded banquet, using replicas of the American flag for napkins at each place setting - all very patriotic, and exciting for Key West.

As the parade was passing by the Dr. Porter home on the corner of Duval and Caroline Street, a family friend looked up to see Will Porter, age seven, up on the high mansart roof dancing and prancing joyfully to the band music in his white night shirt. I can still see him up there now.

When Will Porter was in his mid-twenties and his parents were away on a trip, he and a group of local young bloods somehow managed to rent or reserve

W. R. Porter, "Billy"
about 8 years old.

the entire Elks Club (now Hard Rock Cafe) for a stag party, hiring and transporting a group of dancers for their general entertainment.

When a neighbor got wind of this affair in progress, he called the police who immediately arrived to raid the party. Most of the male participants quickly and nimbly evacuated through windows and back doors - but not Billy Porter. He stayed put with the girls who didn't

The Jefferson Hotel

President Grant welcome parade down Duval Street

know where to run or how to hide. Later, his mother Louisa was horrified hearing the lurid details on their return. But his father Dr. Porter, while not approving openly, patted him on the shoulder for not being a deserter or running away from the face of social disaster.

Both his parents were relieved and delighted when he met my future grandmother, Grace Dorgan when on a bank business trip to Mobile. They hoped that marrying this lovely girl would finally settle him down and it did– almost.

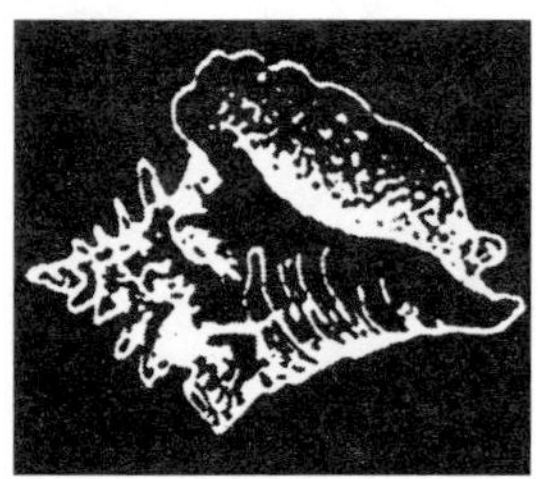

Love Lane Key West

In Deep

There is buried treasure in Heritage House's old back garden. Perhaps it lies in the vicinity of the huge elephant-gray barked Spanish lime, or near the native almond tree whose red, orange and magenta leaves masquerade in late spring as Indian summer. Or perhaps it lies buried somewhere near the foot of or under the giant gumbo limbo that has been entwined amicably for well over a hundred years with a sea grape tree. Somewhere in this ancient back garden or along its side drive, is buried a Spanish treasure, or so legends insisted!

In the early 1880s my grandfather, Will Porter, and a group of his friends, all boys about twelve to fourteen, came hunting in the dark of night down the side driveway off Caroline Street. Several yards in, near the huge Spanish lime tree they paused and stood clustered together, half a dozen or so, around a shared kerosene lantern. Treasure hunting by day held no magic. This midnight search was much more fun and exciting. They paused in the dark huddled tightly together near the side of the then unoccupied sea captains' house getting their bearings. Suddenly they felt an ominous trembling beneath their feet and then with a crack of splintering wood giving way, like a magician's disappearing act, the entire group of boys suddenly vanished into thin air. A moment later they found themselves up to their necks in a long-abandoned cesspool whose aged cover had given way under their combined weight. The boys, once they had regained their senses, climbed slowly out of the muck and without a word, disbanded and headed in different directions for their homes.

Pop said it would be the last hunt that his generation would ever attempt to find the lost Spanish treasure of Heritage House Gardens.

Wash Day Key West by Marion Winter

Still Open Sesame

Well, Jerry," the voice of William Randolph Porter, President of the First National Bank of Key West (now the First Union, on lower Duval Street), reverberated in friendly authority. He had just called from his hotel room at the Great Northern in New York City to his Vice-President, Jerry Trevor in Key West.

"I'm sure you must have heard the President," he said, "we'll have to close the bank."

Newly elected FDR had just made his first nationwide radio broadcast announcing the number one step in his plan called "The New Deal" that was to help bail the U. S. out of the Great Depression: all U. S. banks were to close for ten days while the Government examined the whole sick U. S. economy.

"But, Mr. Porter," protested Trevor, his voice rising Conch style in protest, "we can't do that! They've already lined up around the block to put money INTO the bank."

It was a typical 'outlandish' Key West reaction. All over the U. S. at that moment doors were slamming as people rushed out headed for their banks to withdraw the last of their precious savings. Who really knew for sure when the banks would open again? It was deep depression March, 1933.

"Mr. Porter, please sir," explained Jerry pleadingly, "all the spongers and fishermen insist this is the only safe place they have to keep their savings. We can't lock them out and let them down now at a time like this!"

Porter considered for a moment and then agreed with conviction, "Very well, Jerry," he said, "so be it! We'll stay open."

In all probability, The First National Bank of Key West was one of the only banks in the entire U.S.A. that did!

The First National Bank of Key West - now First Union Bank

All Aboard!

As a child, climbing aboard the Flagler East Coast Railroad in Key West was like entering a magical side door to paradise. The heady scent of fresh starched linen, of polished brass and crystal, and waxed and glowing mahogany was intoxicating. The train (the Silver Meteor to New York, and the Orange Blossom Special back to Florida, as I remember) left Key West in the late afternoon wrapped in a golden orange sunset that reflected in the waters gliding by below. Passengers had an aerial view of molten sea, distant mangrove keys and huge billowing and flaming cloud formations over a limitless expanse of horizon and water.

We would first quickly settle belongings into our comforable compartment and then head for the club car, where the delicious sound of ice tinkling in highball glasses of sparkling ginger-ale mixed with the clickity click sound of the train wheels. Traveling with my beloved grandmother, Grace Porter, was as near to heaven as I could ever get. As I leaned back against her shoulder with her arm around me, I knew we were off to high adventure together. I remember with delight settling into the cozy and luxurious sleeping compartments, all fresh-scented comfort and neatness. I could look

H. M. Flagler, October 26, 1911

out the windows from the berth at night to see the mysterious world going by outside, like a view of Eden, while inside, we were in its moving clickity-clicking heart, snug and secure.

I remember the excitement of arriving at the station and getting off the train in New York, through clouds of warm steam (I guess from other trains — Flagler's cars were electric). The huge, vaulted-ceilinged station with its brisk, suddenly cooler air was such a thrill and contrast from Florida's sultry September heat. The crowds all around us were full of bustle and purpose and seemed electrically charged.

Sometimes with me in tow, my Grandfather would head for the Grand Central station's famous Oyster Bar and seat us on stools. Pop would be wearing a look of vast pleasure and expectation, like a ship-wrecked sailor knowing that he was about to be rescued, he would order the waiter to bring on oysters and to continue to bring on oysters until he told him to stop. After several dozen passionately enjoyed mollusks, Pop would hold up his hand like a policeman stopping a stream of traffic signalling: "Enough!" We would then get up and proceed hand in hand— Pop with a look of satisfied bliss — to catch an open top taxi uptown to join my grandmother who had gone ahead to the hotel. How wonderful and extraordinary it was to ride in one of those open-topped yellow cabs driving up Broadway at night, especially beautiful since I was too young to read the lighted signs and could just be dazzled by their splendor!

The Porters usually stayed at the Great Northern, on 56th or 57th Street, near 5th Avenue. It was a favorite Mecca for Southerners visiting New York City in those days,

Florida East Coast Railroad

and now, I am told, by Latin Americans. It had views of Central Park and was near the Plaza Hotel, where my grandmother would often meet friends for lunch or tea in its luxurious Palm Room. I'll never forget the small orchestra and the strolling violinist playing over our shoulders and down our spines: "Vilia, oh Vilia, You Witch of the Wood," and "Play, Gypsy, Play," and "I Dreamt I Dwelt in Marble Halls, Servants and Slaves by my Si-hi-hide," or the latest tunes from Broadway — "Tea For Two" or "I Wanna Be Loved By You, Just You." As Noel Coward said later about his own songs, "Strange how potent cheap music can be!" Does anyone remember the songs "The Orange Blossom Special" or "Shuffle Off to Buffalo"?

✳   ✳   ✳

I know I have mixed together in my 5 to 10 year old memory the Penn and the Grand Central Stations. They were both fascinating worlds. Was it the Penn that has the beautiful ceiling of star-lighted constellations and the Grand Central that hosted the Oyster Bar?

Big Guns
1916

The Admiral was holding forth at Will and Grace Porter's dinner table about his many military exploits and adventures. He had his audience impressed and captivated as he boomed in a "long ago and far away" voice: "When I was captain of the four-masted Brigantine "Triumph," anchored in the harbour of Moscow..."

Jessie's dinner companion, a young, blonde ensign, freshly minted and hatched from Annapolis, was so entranced that he forgot his humble status and blurted out:

"But Admiral, I thought Moscow was an inland city!"

The Admiral's eagle-beaked profile with it's immense white bottle brush eyebrows pivoted slowly around toward him, his eyes zeroing in on the hapless target like two highly polished cannons.

"Have you ever been there?" he growled.

"No sir," quailed the now pale and shaken ensign, "No never have, sir."

"Well then," continued the Admiral, turning back to his audience and clearing his throat: "As I was saying - when I was Captain of the four-masted brigantine "Triumph" anchored in the harbour of Moscow..."

Commodore Porter's epaulets, Dr. Mudd's shell box, William Curry carving set. Heritage House collection

Smoking

L ife in families can sometimes resemble a big looped roller-coaster. One generation steps off and the other gets on. It can be a scary ride sometimes.

My grandfather smoked like a steam locomotive. He loved cigars.

Every Christmas the Cuban President (Dictator), Fulgencio Batista y Zaldivar, sent him, as president of the bank, a big cedar box of Corona Coronas from Havana with his name, W.R. Porter, on the box label and on each ring. I used to treasure them and wear them on my finger as a little girl. My grandfather, "Pop," would say we were "engaged." He smoked these Cuban cigars and their excellent Key West progeny with gusto all his life. He smoked so much that his throat and gums bled. It worried him terribly, but it didn't stop him. Finally he was sure he had throat cancer.

One fall, when he and my grandmother arrived in New York for their seasonal visit, he was coughing and clearing his throat so often that my grandmother, worried as well, insisted he see a specialist.

"It's better to face it if something is really wrong, Will," she said,

"than to go on worrying and worrying and do nothing until it is too late to do anything at all." So with her urging, he made an appointment to see one of the leading throat specialists in the city.

Big Mama and I made a point of being back at the hotel when she knew he would return from the doctor's visit.

In he came seeming to float on gossamer wings, almost dancing on air. He was a short stocky man, with an imposing portly banker's presence (tummy). To see him highstepping like a ballet dancer was disarming. "Well how did it go?" asked my grandmother, already guessing from his elated appearance and body language that the answer was positive. Pop almost crooned his reply. "The doctor said I have a Nervous Operatic Throat," he reported joyfully.

"What did he charge?" asked my grandmother suspiciously. "Oh, three hundred dollars," Pop replied cheerfully. "Three hundred dollars!" repeated my grandmother in shock. This was during the Great Depression between 1932 and 34. "You call that doctor's office and tell them you want another diagnosis for three hundred dollars, other than a Nervous Operatic Throat!"

Years later I was sitting in the elevated examining chair of a throat specialist in Holland. I had been living with my family in the Hague near the North Sea. The cold wet wind had given me a perpetual cough and sore throat. I was also a smoker trying to cut back on cigarettes with tiny little cigars called "Schrimel Pannicks" — a potent substitute — enough to make me worry constantly about getting throat cancer.

The doctor came up for air having been submerged with a long tubular flash light, viewing my throat. He looked relieved. "Well, it is certainly inflamed and swollen," he said as he straightened up, "but no sign of polyps or lesions," he continued. "I have many patients who come to me with this same condition. Many of them are singers — particularly opera singers."

I left his office on gossamer wings, almost dancing on air, but wondering what his bill would be for my "Nervous Operatic Throat."

Overseas Highway over Pigeon Key

Perspective

This story should be a comfort to the baby-boomers now arriving at the mid-century of their lives. It certainly comforted my grandfather.

*   *   *

Grace considered her downcast husband with sympathy and compassion. She had never seen him looking quite so desolate or blue. His usual high energy and forceful personality seemed utterly deflated, as wilted and flat as a hot air balloon.

"I know it feels like the end of the world, Will," she said with sympathy. "Arriving at fifty must be quite a jolt."

He was sitting in his handsome lion-crested and carved mahogany rocking chair in their living room. This 'throne' was often his "exerciser." He could release static energy between rocks by clicking his heels together at the high tilt, often managing up to four or five rapid clicks before touching the floor again. But now he sat in dejected immobility.

"My dear," his wife continued, "you must change your perspective. You must look at age from a different point of view." She

Grace Porter – 1910

patted his arm with affection. "If you think of fifty from a young man's point of view, well, fifty does seem ancient. But, Will, if you perceive fifty from the vantage point of an older man, say one of seventy-five or more .." she paused for emphasis, "then fifty becomes just the babyhood of older age!"

Grace Porter – 1896

Big Mama
Grace Dorgan Porter

Hobson's Choice
Privacy
Beautiful Babe
Looks
Clouds

Hobson's Choice
(American Style)

The pretty and vivacious Dorgan girls surrounded Mammy, looking amused but also a little anxious.

"Mammy," they insisted, "can't you remember anything? Anything?"

The year was 1898 and The Hero of the Spanish American War, Lieutenant J.G. Richard Hobson, was coming to dinner that evening. He was back home in Mobile after a national war bond selling tour that had taken him to every nook and cranny in the United States.

Hobson was a tall, attractive, blond young man, a graduate of Annapolis, and according to all the enthusiastic Hearst and Pulitzer newspaper coverage, spectacularly brave and daring. So brave and daring, in fact, that he had become the idol of almost every girl in the country and the ideal catch to every blue-blooded American mother with marriageable daughters.

Plays had been written, songs were being sung ("I'll See You In C.U.B.A."), balls and parties were given in his honor. Everywhere, whole towns and villages turned out en masse to hear the popular young Naval officer speak. Hobson's "choice" was assumed to be any lucky girl he wanted to honor with a dance, or a proposal of marriage, or capture with a beckoning of his white-gloved finger and a smile of his very white teeth. But, sadly, the spoils of war had begun to have their effect and rub off on the gregarious Hobson, and he had become somewhat spoiled himself in the process.

The Dorgan and Hobson families had known each other since they were children, a generation earlier.

Grace Dorgan Porter – c.1890

Jessie Dorgan, Grace's mother — my great grandmother — had felt it her duty, not to say her pleasure, to invite him to dinner as part of his homecoming to Mobile. Richard had, knowing and remembering the attractive Dorgan girls, accepted with alacrity.

"Please, Mammy, do try to remember at least some of his speech!" Grace and Una persisted, a bit impatiently now. After all, Mammy had gone as she had been asked, to hear him speak at the City Hall the night before. She had sat up in the peanut gallery reserved for the black folks, with much resigned dignity and patience — Patience that had been stretched to its utmost. Hobson,

Mammy – 1875

as the girls had heard through the grapevine and so expected, had gone on and on about his adventures and exploits, elaborating and embellishing each and every detail: how he had gone (one would have thought alone, though a chief petty officer and six crew members were with him) in the dark of night sailing stealthily into the narrow entrance of Santiago Bay on the southern coast of Cuba; how threatening the Spanish fleet had looked lying in wait in the dark; the shore batteries above them on the ramparts ready to blast him out of the water; how violent the explosion had been that he had set off that sank the U.S. Carrier Merrimac, lighting and giving away their position to the enemy; his ensuing capture and imprisonment by the Spanish, and his final rescue by the Great American Navy.

In spite of the Hearst newspaper reports and their emblazoned headlines declaring that the entire Spanish fleet had been bottled up in Santiago Bay by this brilliantly strategic maneuver, "bottled up" was not quite accurate it was later learned, though it did look great in print. Unfortunately, Lieutenant Hobson had begun to believe the press raves and aggrandizement about himself, along with the public, brave though he assuredly was and undoubtedly had been.

"Mammy, he must have said SOMETHING you can remember!" the girls pleaded. Their plan had been to send Mammy to hear Richard speak and report back to them so that at dinner that evening they could pretend to have heard the illustrious Hobson, without having to go and be bored the entire evening beforehand. Mammy pursed her lips and shook her head, searching her memory and mumbling.

Lt. Hobson

"He talked and he talked — he sure did talk — two and a half hours he did talk."

"But what did he say Mammy? Please, do remember something we can use as dinner conversation tonight!"

"It's the Lord's truth," Mammy shook her head. "I don't rightly remember exactly much of anything he say." Then triumphantly, "except," she paused for emphasis, "HE SURE DID RECOM-MEND HIMSELF HIGH!"

The Battleship Maine

Privacy

Back in the days when privacy was not only considered a right but also a sacrament, Henry Baldwin had been an old friend of the Porters for well over 15 years. Charming, urbane, worldly and amusing, his visits to Key West involving my grandfather's First National Bank had become occasions that both Grace and Will Porter looked forward to with pleasure.

In spite of Henry's sociability and charm, there remained, however, a pool of mystery in the make-up of this attractive man; a recess of containment no one had ever dared intrude upon. In all the years that the Porters had known him, he had never mentioned even once a salient and important fact or discussed its cause . . . that he was missing his left arm.

One evening after a delicious dinner of pompano almondine, Grace found herself and her guest sitting together on the front porch in its big comfortable wicker rockers. The night was filled with fireflies and the air perfect, neither warm nor cool. Their after dinner port had been heartwarming and relaxing and Grace, in spite of the decorum of the day never to intrude uninvited into a friend's private affairs, found herself irresistibly concerned and curious as the feeling of relaxed sociability overwhelmed her.

"Henry," she began leaning towards him and touching his completed right arm resting on the arm of the rocker nearby, "I know you don't like to talk about it since you have never mentioned it in all the years we've known you." She could sense his head turn toward her in the soft darkness and his neck stiffen slightly.

"I know you don't like to talk about it," she repeated nervously and then once launched plunged over the cataract. "But you know

Grace Dorgan Porter – 1900

how interested we are ,and how fond we are of you that I simply can't help wondering how in all these years you have never said one word, never once mentioned your arm - how you lost it." She could sense his gaze now turned directly toward her, but she breathed deeply and continued, "I don't want to pry, so please don't say anything if you don't want to, but I can't help wondering — fond as we are of you — how did it happen?" She paused and then said very earnestly, "If you tell me Henry, I promise, I'll never mention it again — never."

He leaned toward her and responded quietly. "You're right, Grace," he said, "I don't like to talk about it. But if I tell you, do you promise we'll never talk about it again?"

"Never!" she agreed fervently. "I'll never mention it, not one word, not ever again."

"Very well," he said resignedly, "I'll tell you." He paused and then almost blurted out — "It was bitten off!"

Henry came back to Key West many times for many visits with the Porters but Grace, true to her word, kept her promise. She never mentioned it again.

Beautiful Babe

G race Porter and Etta Patterson are visiting together on Grace's front porch on Duval Street. It is Friday. Miss Etta is the not-quite middle-aged spinster daughter of General Patterson and lives around the corner on Caroline Street. Her two elder sisters have married and left the island but Etta has stayed on to take care of her widowed father. She has a pleasant singing voice and a lively curious nature. Her one burst of freedom had been to study voice for a few months in Italy when she was twenty. She makes "Delicious Divinity," a Key West candy, to perfection, creates beautiful flower arrangements and is an active Women's Club member and supporter. She sings at all their socials. Her favorite song is "Oh, Promise Me."

Part of their conversation goes like this:

Grace: Thursday afternoon, yesterday, was the maid's afternoon off.

Etta (always curious): What happened?

Grace: Well there was a knock on the back door so I went to

The Key West Women's Club, Genevieve Warren President at center, Minnie Porter Harris lower left

answer it.

Etta: Who was it? What happened?

Grace: It was a scruffy-looking egg dealer and he was quite drunk.

Etta: Oh, my! Grace, that's awful!

Grace: He was swaying back and forth on the door step, then reached into a sack and produced one egg and held it up in front of my nose and said, "Wanna buy shum eggs, Beautiful Babe?' (She imitates his slurred speech).

Etta (shocked): I hope you slammed the door in his face and called the police! I hope you had him arrested!

Grace: I did nothing of the sort, Etta!

Etta: What DID you do?

Grace: I bought every egg he had! I haven't been called "Beautiful Babe"' in twenty years!

*　　*　　*

For a very long time Miss Etta had a delightful beau who would come down to visit her once or twice a year. Each time everyone, including Etta, would hope that he would finally pop the question and ask her to marry him. Her friend Grace, who said she didn't believe in giving away advice unless it was paid for — "otherwise," she said, "it's never appreciated" — finally couldn't resist advising Etta.

"Sooner or later the excitement and tumult of a new marriage calms down, and it does calm down, Etta," she said. "Then what begins to really count, what means the most, are the things that you share with another person; what you remember together. In other words it's the familiars that really count. So, Etta," Grace paused for emphasis, "you had better start familiarizing yourself."

Miss Etta's beau never did propose, but Etta remained an optimist all her life.

"Porch talk"– a favorite Key West sport

Looks

Mother always said, "I feel so sorry for women who think they have to depend on their looks for social acceptance and/or financial success. Their fear about growing older must be dreadful. Thank God I was not born a great beauty. I'll never have to worry about fading!"

*   *   *

Her mother, Grace Porter, agreed, but felt a little differently about looks. "What you are born with is up to God and family heredity," she said, "until the age of forty. After forty, looks can be what you make of them yourself."

*   *   *

One day Grace caught Jessie in full flight, absorbed in a myriad of projects and people. "Jessie," she said in her amused Southern (Mobile) voice. "I know you think you are being selfless in not paying more attention to how you look . . . no make-up, hair flying in all directions. But it's really being very selfish. It's not you who has to look at yourself. Other people do. So, my dear, won't you please consider improving the view?"

In the hot and humid Key West summer I remember Big Mama lamenting to Pop: "Oh Will, if you had only taken me just 10° further south we wouldn't have to pretend to civilization!"

Grace & Jessie Porter – c.1912

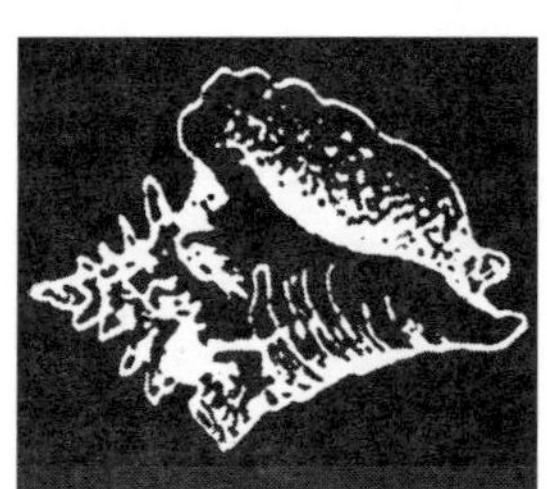

Clouds

on't you get tired of living in such flat country?" asked a visitor at lunch.

Grace Porter and her guest, a lady from Baltimore, were sitting on the upper deck of the houseboat, Idler, anchored in a pool of azure water a mile off the northwest side of the Island. The boat, swinging languidly on its two anchor moorings was slowly turning in a soft sea breeze. Gulls, man-o-war birds and pelicans floated high up in the air currents while the air itself felt like feathers against their skin.

"Flat?" responded Grace in surprise.

All around them, but particularly over the Gulf Stream, great billowing cumulus clouds had built up past twenty thousand feet, luminous in pinks and lavenders against a dazed blue sky.

"But we're not flat here at all," Grace said. "Just look at those clouds!" she invited her guest. "Those are our mountains, and they change every day."

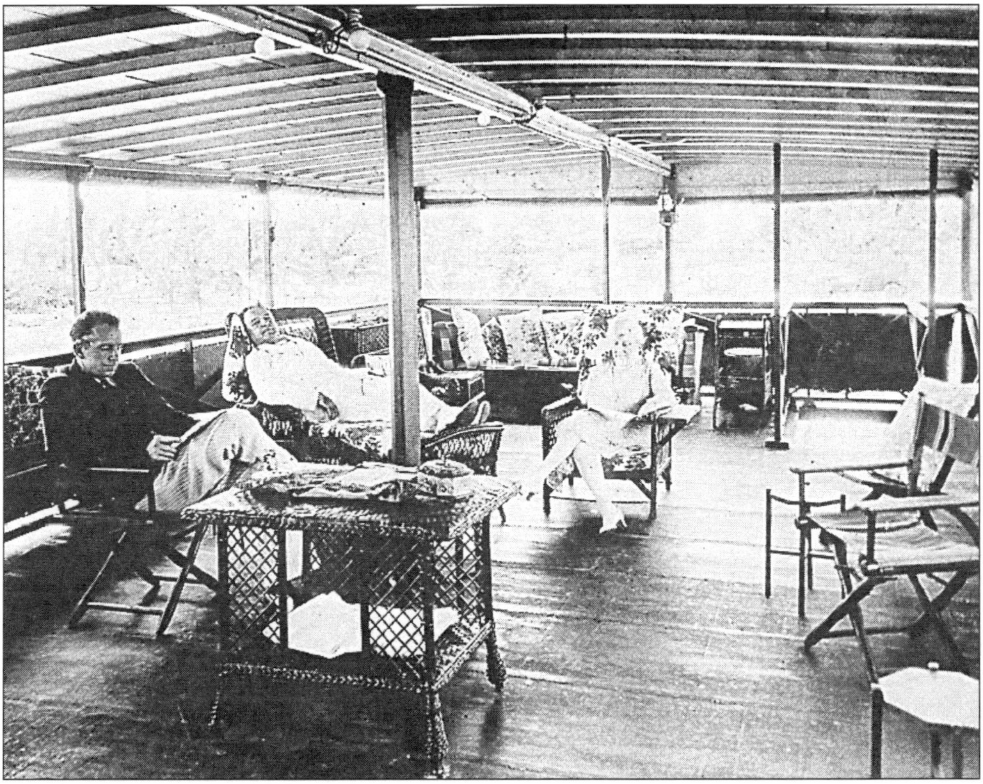

The Porters with their guest Juan Tripp - Father of Commercial Aviation (Pan Am) – on the upper deck of the house boat Idler.

*   *   *

I turned up Duval from Caroline the other afternoon and there in the sky suspended directly over the street, was a ten mile high replica of Mount Fujiyama floating solo with not another cloud in sight! It's snowy sides were shining mother of pearl cascading down from it's cone-shaped peak to its base swaddled in pink, salmon and lavender, and all of this was miraculously hovering above our main street's silvery rooftops! What a vision!! What a surprise!! What a sight!!!

Left to right: my old playmate Barbara Bowser Schleck with a friend, center leading artists Arnold Blanche and Doris Lee, writer Benedict Thielen and Betty Garnette

Key West Personalities

Captain Eddy
The Last of the Key West Pirates
Mike and the Mermaid
Hebe Mennor
Distant Drum
Killie the Horse
Run for Your Life
Lady Godiva
Autumn for Mrs. Barnes
The Southernmost Castle

Captain Eddy and Jeane with a gigantic manta ray. c.1936

Captain Eddy

Captain Eddy's other name was Bra Saunders. He was a well-known fishing guide on the island and had taught Ernest Hemingway how to fish in Key West waters. He is also credited with being the prototype for the character Harry Morgan in Hemingway's To Have and Have Not. *The picture illustrating this story shows Captain Eddy and myself when I was 10 or so. The huge Manta Ray had been caught by our friends the Bentleys who were visiting on their yacht here. Captain Eddy was their guide. They called us to come see this "denizen of the deep" after church one Sunday. I'm still dressed for Sunday School. I don't remember who the boy was. Perhaps he is Captain Eddie's son.*

*   *   *

Rum wasn't the only thing smuggled in from Cuba during prohibition days: illegal aliens, especially the Chinese, were, too. A popular Key West waterfront character, Captain Eddy knew all about it first hand. He was a weather-beaten, appealing, tough sea salt, rum runner, fisherman, smuggler, lover, drinker and storyteller who hung out on the waterfront at Sloppy Joe's and at Fisherman's Cafe down on Caroline.

"Yes, sir," mused Captain Eddy. "They used to think I was Jesus Christ, they used to kiss my hand — poor devils."

Through Cuban underground connections, a rendezvous spot would be chosen outside Havana to pick up the live cargo at night. The cost of flight and delivery to the U.S. shore was $250 per man — a fortune then — perhaps the lifetime savings of many individuals to invest in one man's delivery to paradise.

A dozen Chinese could be stuffed like sardines into the hold of an average fishing boat. They would be put into potato sacks if a Coast Guard vessel came within a mile away on the horizon. If the Coast Guard got any closer, the sacks were tied at the top. If they got nearer than a half mile, the sack and contents were dumped off the side, overboard.

"Taking no chances," he explained matter of factly. "But most of the time, we got them to shore." Captain Eddy looked pleased with himself. "We'd sail all night. Just before dawn, we'd let them out of the hold up on deck. They'd see palm trees, a beach, America! We'd come in close to shore, as close as possible without grounding. Then the Chinese would all jump overboard yelling, 'F l o r - i d a! F l o r - i d a!' They were so happy, happy," he said. "They used to try to kiss my hand. Later that day, they would discover they had arrived on the other end of Cuba, near Guantanamo or some place near. It took the same length of time to get there as the Keys. But most of the time, we got them to Florida okay," he said looking virtuous.

*   *   *

"My wife was tired of me being at sea so much. Getting tired of me too, maybe. So I bought her a great big mirror in the Havana flea market. It had all kinds of gold flowers and carved angels around it, and we nailed it up on the ceiling over our bed. Boy, oh boy! What a change! Night and day, day and night. I've even stopped fishing for awhile."

*   *   *

"Fishing: We had been going out, but catchin' nothin'. Thems fishes is real smart. Them's educated fish. Them fish must go to night school."

- Albert Atwell, a friend of Captain Eddy's and mine.

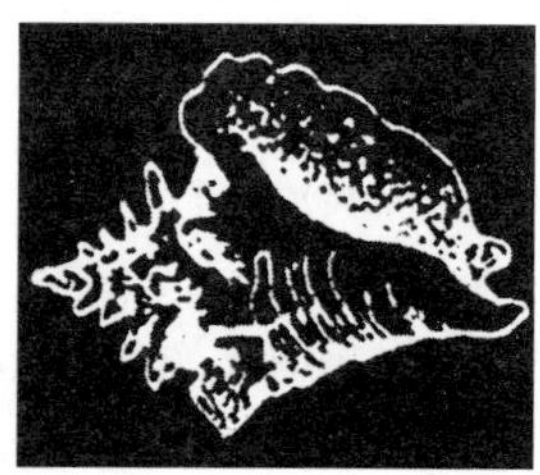

The Last of the Key West Pirates

Some of my ancestors and collateral relatives (Commodore David Porter for one) were pirate fighters — from the word go, so in this story, prejudice as well as genes and chromosomes do out!

Key West has always had its share of pirates, even extending into the present day. I am sure that several of the bars in town house their reincarnated spirits where they come to drink and carouse as they did in former lives, as worthless and as derelict a bunch as ever.

This story relates to a home-grown pirate, one that still lived on Whitehead Street in the late 20s, early 30s. We won't use his whole name because he came from good Key West stock who are still here, and he lived in a big West Indian colonial house across the street and up Whitehead from what is now the Green Parrot Bar. The location of his house is now a parking lot.

Harry B., as I'll call him, became a pirate at a very early age and at the very tail end of piracy, when it had become quite hazardous but was no longer a very lucrative occupation. He had quickly

Whitehead Street Pirate's House was at center left

picked up most of that profession's bad habits: drinking, laziness, and free spending of what he had inherited or currently made as a fisherman. He was ill-kempt, careless, and he had never married. He drank daily and nightly at the local bar where he was always late in paying his bills.

His drinking cronies claimed he had stashed money in the ground under his house, for he hardly spent any except on booze. His house was in terrible condition, badly needing repair and painting. Due to the Depression, so many houses on the Island were in that same dilapidated condition, or almost as bad, that it wasn't considered unusual. What was unusual was the giant trumpet vine growing up the side of the house beginning to cover the roof. It was as gnarled and dense as a huge fist in thickness and was slowly engulfing the roof and the entire building. When it was in flower, hundreds of big cream colored blossoms hung down like bells or trumpets, perfuming the whole neighborhood on summer evenings.

On this last night, our pirate spent the evening drinking in his favorite tavern, and then staggered home to bed and to sleep. Just before dawn when the Key West roosters and cats were having a last minute promenade and local fishermen were headed down Whitehead Street to their boats, there was heard an awesome and terrible sound: the scream of ancient timbers splitting and cracking and giving way. Then the whole house, in agonizingly slow motion, shook and trembled and finally collapsed to the ground under the weight of the enormous vine. When the dense cloud of dust had settled it materialized into a huge leaf-covered pyramid of debris, vine, and flowers. Only golden dust clouds, swirling in the early morning sunlight, signaled in rising shafts of light the demise of the Last of the Key West Pirates.

KEY WEST CHARACTERS TO REMEMBER

Big Annie on Emma Street
Caladonia
Cucu Baba or Bobo
Jew Fish
Black Jack
Julia Rio
King Fish
King Conch
Che Che
Ingar Sweeting
Cabbage Head

coral vine

Mike and the Mermaid

A favorite childhood hero and friend, Mike Shine, to my great admiration was as strong, sinewy and sun-scorched as a stretched sisal rope. One theory holds that night-people have larger eyes than day-people, and that day-people's eyes are often more squinted than night-people's, especially against the Florida sun. Certainly, this was true of Mike. His high cheek bones and tight, weather-beaten, dark-tanned skin also gave him the cast and look of a wise and ageless American Indian.

He could jack rabbit himself up the trunks of palm trees in a flash – barefoot, the outside of his feet turned inward like a vice – and lop off a fresh milk coconut that would fall with a muffled thump to the grass. Mike would drop gracefully down and with another masterful swoosh of his machete cut off the top, and with a flourish present me with a natural green cup of cool, slightly syrupy coconut milk. Nothing has ever tasted better than Mike's Coconut Milk. "Good for everything," he would say.

And Mike was a wonderful storyteller. He would regale me with stories of bandit skirmishes, tales of his capture in Mexico in

Mike's Mermaid by Susie dePoo Zuzak

the days of Pancho Villa. I was never sure just which side he was on, the American side or the side of the bandits, the "Mexicos" as he called them. Both were so wily and romantic. Mike would always be captured, sleep on a bed of straw, and always barely manage to escape execution just before dawn. I suspect he was really on the "Mexicos" side at heart. They were such rascals.

Mike's little caretaker cottage was set out at the Biological Station, as it was then called, at the head of the Island under tall coconut palms. It was surrounded by Spanish cork trees and set in a large grove of big Australian pines that had sprung up from hedges and through which the breeze blew and made a wonderful shushing sound like soft rain falling. The property, owned by one of my grandfather's companies, had a deep tidal "kraal" cut out of the native coral rock where turtles were kept for feasts and special occasions. A high white tower in the center of the property was full of stuffed bird specimens, herons, that looked out regally through wall slots to the Cow Key Channel.

This land, I believe, had originally been destined for Flagler's Casa Marina Hotel, before he changed his mind to build it nearer town. Pop had bought it, and later, at the beginning of World War II, he gave a considerable part of it to the U.S. government to build the big Naval Hospital there.

But in the days before that, we kept the family houseboat, the Idler, out there from January until the official storm season began in June or July. The comfortable but top-heavy houseboat, originally a Navy barge that had been enlarged and covered, and enlarged again until the Depression put an end to its transformation, would then be towed to the Garrison Bight for shelter from possible hurricanes.

Once during those spring months, when the air was fresh and light as feathers and blew continuously, Mike built me an enormous four-by-six foot box kite made from balsa wood and brown paper bags. When we launched it, it stayed aloft over Cow Key in the tradewinds lashed to the boat dock rail for over three months! Some kind of Guinness Book Record, I think. (Shouldn't there be wind generators out there to create electric power for the city? There is always a breeze blowing at Cow Key, as I remember.)

I remember, too, that one afternoon it rained fish. They flopped around on the thick Bermuda grass quite alive, staring up at the mysterious fleeting cloud that had somehow picked them up, probably by waterspout, and then jettisoned them on land. They looked up as surprised as I felt.

My friend Mike had a secret life that I think only I knew about. As a solitary bachelor he had one Great Love — and she was a mermaid. Sitting under his palm tree together drinking coconut milk, he told me about how he had found and lost her.

One night, he said, unable to sleep, he had taken his dinghy out to check his crawfish traps. There was a full moon as he rowed out into the Cow Key Channel. It was such a calm and beautiful night. The phosphorous were unswirling themselves in violet cosmic whirls on the surface of the shallows, and the moonlit waters were as full of enchanted lights below the surface as above in the sky. It was then, in this magic moment, that he saw her! She was sitting on a small exposed sand bank next to the channel, languid and beautiful. In the clear moonlight he could even see the color of her long red-gold hair, and that she was combing it with a tortoise shell comb. Her neck was swan-like, and the skin of her shoulders and back was as pale and rosy pink as a shell's heart.

"So as not to frighten her away or warn her, I dug my oars deep into the water just as silent and carefully as I could and came up behind her," he remembered. "She was too frightened at first even to cry out when I grabbed her with both my arms and pulled her into the boat. I held her for a moment and then I lowered her down onto the floor of the boat. Her long silver tail was trembling as it touched the planks and disappeared under the rear seat. I stood above her, looking down into her frightened eyes. They were magic, the color of blue-green sapphires, as bright as jewels. She began to moan, and then to beg me . . . so pitiful like!" Mike said shaking his head as he remembered the moment. "Please, don't take me to shore!" she whispered. "I can't live on land —— I'll die if you try to keep me on land." She wrung her hands and began to weep, looking up at me pleadingly - she was so beautiful! Finally, I could stand it no longer, so I picked her up again and very carefully I lowered her back into the water. She was so grateful! She murmured, "Thank you — thank you!" and then she sank slowly into the depths of the channel, reaching her arms up and looking up towards me, saying good-bye and smiling. The moonlight on her soft, beautiful face got dimmer and dimmer as she sank into the depths and finally disappeared."

"Sometimes, at night, I can hear her. . . ." he said, looking out toward the channel. "I can hear her out there. Singing to me."

Mike and Jeane checking his traps.

Hebe Mennor

S he began life in Baltimore as (plain) Jane and through various life incarnations ended up Hebe (Goddess of the Hunt). She had a high-bridged aristocratic nose, large beautiful hyper-thyroid green eyes, arched eyebrows and wavy cropped marcelled hair that fell sweetly on the pale nape of her long neck. She was a beauty.

Somewhere along the line she had hennaed her hair a full sunrise copper that was a World War I 'must' in fashion. It remained that color until her personal hairdresser enlisted in the WACS at the beginning of World War II.

Hebe was devastated. "What shall I do? What shall I do?" she lamented.

Finally, inspiration struck: "I know! I know! I'll let my hair go white and WEAR red!"

Her third? – or fourth? - husband was Captain Walter Mennor, Commandant of the Key West Naval Station in the 30s. It was the period between wars, doldrums to the Navy with plenty of leisure time to socialize. Hebe and the Captain entertained often and with style. Their parties were the social events of the Island and were held on the large comfortable porches of the Commandant's Quarters that is now called "The Little White House."

Captain Mennor was a very tall six foot four or five, handsome, dark-haired man with an active and tolerant sense of humor. Humor that stood him in good stead with Hebe. She would regale their guests with stories of her past lives and adventures: "When I was riding to the hounds with Peter in Sussex (or Kent) . . . " Mennor would aside, "She's talking about number three, Lord Palmer," he would explain.

"We were tiger hunting in Bengal one night . . . "

Mennor would helpfully supply, "That's Sidney, an Australian," or "Woolly the writer," or "Pierre de la Rocohaut, the French Nobel Laureate chemist."

Hebe and Walter seemed to have found a very happy and congenial marriage that lasted many years until his death. Hebe then settled into a small apartment just off Fifth Avenue in the 60s. Navy widow's pensions were not very bountiful in those lean days before World War II, but small space made her parties even more intimate and fun.

When we moved into the hotel across from the Algonquin, the Royalton, I believe, getting ready to go to Australia, Hebe would walk energetically down all of Fifth Avenue to visit me once or twice a week. It was her "constitutional." She strode, not walked, head high, wearing a floating cape and swinging an elegant cane or umbrella. She was a parade in one.

Just before we left, she announced jubilantly, "I've decided to marry Henry. He's been asking me for years. I've decided to finally give him what he's always wanted!"

She was seventy-six and the bride wore red.

Distant Drum

etty Garnett, along with half the town, would head for the post office on Simonton Street on hot afternoons to mail letters. It was more of an excuse just to stand in the cool, glimmering shade of the marbled interior to cool off, and while there, to socialize — get together with the other half of overheated Key West.

On this particularly sultry afternoon, she ran into Judge L . . . mopping his brow and mailing packets. They greeted each other warmly. Betty was a bright ex-newspaper woman from Washington, D.C., who had been, along with her husband Bert, part of Bob Allen and Drew Pierson's Washington Merry-Go-Round group. She was known for her bright mind and sharp wit.

Judge L . . . , though considerably deaf, had a reputation for being one of the best judges in the county — though with his hearing problem, people often wondered how he acquired, other than with possible lip-reading, enough information from oral testimony to make judgments. Still he did, and very fairly too, for the most part.

After they had greeted each other, the Judge, who had very

Betty and Bert Garnette

large dark eyes rather like Eddie Cantor's and an animated delivery, launched into a joyous accolade about his new hearing aid.

"Look at the size of this!" he demanded, pointing to his ear, wherein resided a small pinkish colored shell. "Hearing aids used to be as big as boxes — so large and cumbersome," he continued, "you had to wire their big batteries under your jacket or on your

144

shirt front. Huge and heavy as a brick." Once launched the Judge went on and on raving about how his new age device could be adjusted to suit the situation: loud when outside at a ball game, lower when you were indoors. He continued, extolling the recent wonders he claimed had changed his entire outlook and life.

"It's more than just a wonderful help," he declared! "It is a working miracle!"

Betty, listening interestedly to this enthusiastic tirade, finally asked him curiously, "What kind is it, Judge?"

The Judge quickly glanced over her shoulder at the large clock on the post office wall and then down at his own wristwatch.

"Four forty-five!" he responded brightly.

East Martello Towers by Wallace Kirke

Killie the Horse

emingway's observation in his book, *Death in the Afternoon*, about the emaciated, doomed horses used in the Spanish bull ring, was that the tragedy of their lives had already taken place before they even arrived in the ring. To be gored, humiliated and often mortally wounded there was really an anti-climax of their past life. He wrote instead that they lent a puppet-like, almost comic element to the scene. (Black comedy indeed!) If this is so, this analogy also applied to a Key West character named "Killie the Horse."

I don't know his real name, I don't think many people in town did. He was a tattered, thin, dingy little man, deeply tanned and scorched as old cracked leather by the Key West sun. His work, when he could get it, was to carry other peoples' unwanted belongings and cast-off debris across the island to the city dump. The dump in the 1930s was then located at the salt ponds off the county road now called Flagler Avenue. A long, long, haul. To do this, he used a wagon made of driftwood and boards, held together with a collection of frayed ropes and rusty nails and bolts. The whole sad contraption was always pulled by a succession of dilapidated and emaciated old horses, as desolate and outcast as their owner. It was heavy, hard, harsh work in the hot Key West sun for both man and beast.

On lazy afternoons after loading his wagon, when the town merchants would be home having their after-lunch siestas, one could hear Killie the Horse's wagon rattling over the exposed Baltimore-brick streets in Old Town. He would be followed by a swarm of island boys on bicycles, wheeling and circling like vultures around their victim, crying and jeering, "Killie the Horse, Killie the Horse." The scene was like an ancient Greek tragedy transported to Depression-day Key West; a drama that would play itself out mercilessly and repeatedly, its anti-hero, Killie the Horse, trapped on the wheel of poverty, could only afford old horses on their final legs. They would last a few short months under the heavy loads and their owner's frustrated and frantic beatings. Then eventually fall under their loads to the bricks, struggle up again goaded by Killie's whip, while the boys swarmed around him taunting and jeering in high pitched voices in sing-song chant: "Killie the Horse, Killie the Horse, Killie the Horse."

Run for Your Life
Harry Reilly

Prologue

Harry Reilly's own story is as interesting as the one I want to tell that follows after it. He was discovered as a young chiropractor-therapist by a member of the Rockefeller family, while he was living and working in the "wilds" of New Jersey in the middle 30s. One of the Rockefellers was suffering from a recurrent and painful muscle/bone condition that Harry was able to treat and relieve. Word spread in the family that he was exceptionally gifted and they all went to him. When Rockefeller Center was being built, the entire fourteenth floor (really the 13th) of the RCA Building was reserved for Harry and became Reilly Health Center. It pioneered therapy dedicated to using natural cures: exercise, nutrition, diet, massage, Jacuzzis, steam bath and sunlight, and was set up primarily for the busy city-bound New Yorker, who is out of touch with the "natural"' world. Soon much of the business community, the theater world and later the U.N. flocked to Reilly's.

One particular group of clients, when asked who had referred them, gave the name Edgar Cayce. This recurrence began to intrigue

Harry & Jessie at Sun and Sand

Reilly to inquire, "Who is this Edgar Cayce?" and he eventually went to meet "The Sleeping Prophet" at his home at Virginia Beach. Reilly found that he and Cayce were very much in rapport. Cayce was prescribing in his trance sessions treatments and cures that Reilly also believed in and practiced.

Cayce gave Harry a past-life reading (a former-life story) which, though not verifiable, was certainly supportive and fascinating. He told Reilly that in a former life he had been a top champion Roman gladiator — one that had mindlessly hacked many, many bodies apart. He said, "In this lifetime it is your Karma (fate) to put bodies back together again."

Seeing Reilly, who was an exuberant Irishman, a taller than six foot man, with broad shoulders and a huge barrel chest, as a Roman gladiator was not difficult. His profile, with its powerful jaw line and a nose that was almost a straight line from his forehead, was an astonishing prototype of a living Caesar straight off a Roman coin. Harry's artist wife, Vera looked like a Roman Matron right off a frieze.

*   *   *

Edward Simpson and Reilly were sitting together on the porch of a little cabaña perched on the sands of Rest Beach. Both men were on vacation here. "If I could think of a way not to hurt my wife and children, damage or ruin their lives — I would do away with myself," Simpson, a successful industrialist, confided to Harry Reilly.

Reilly's robust Irish exuberance and blooming health was in marked contrast to the strained ashen appearance of his companion.

Our lost Rest Beach with cabanas 1934

His experienced eye took in the man's exhausted condition, intuitively and from broad experience. "I can't take it much longer, Harry. Not being able to sleep night after night," his friend continued. "It's worse than being on a torture rack."

Harry listened with sympathy and compassion. His health center in New York City treated many uptight, over-worked executives whose "successes" were ruining their lives with stress. He turned to him sympathetically. "Do you really feel that way so strongly, Edward?" Reilly asked with concern. "I certainly do," the deeply troubled man replied.

Reilly thought for a moment and then said, "Very well, I can tell you how you can do it." Edward looked surprised, and then very pleased. With a look of vast relief, he leaned forward, listening to Reilly attentively.

"Rent a car and drive up the Keys," said Reilly. "Pick out the most godforsaken spot you can find, with no one around. Wear a sweat shirt and shorts. Bring along a flask of water, so you won't get dehydrated too soon. Now get out of the car, and start to run!" He paused to look at his friend. "Run and run and run! Run until you drop. Then pick yourself up and run some more. You're in poor shape, and not so young any more. Your heart can't take it. Sooner or later you'll have a heart attack that will finish you off quickly. Your family will never know your intentions."

Edward touched Reilly on the shoulder. "Thank you my friend!" said the grateful executive.

Two days passed while Reilly waited anxiously for news of Edward. Finally the phone rang and an exuberant voice boomed in greeting. "Harry, here I am, still! And never better! When can we talk? I have much to tell you."

When they met each other an hour later on the beach, Simpson looked like a different person. Besides being bright pink turning to a new tan, his whole being seemed to be recharged with energy and life. "What happened? Tell me," smiled Reilly, looking as though he already knew. "Well, old man," said Edward, "I did exactly what you told me to do. I ran like Hell, from six, early morning, until eleven. Finally came to a fisherman's cottage and begged a glass of water. I'd already finished up the flask I had brought with me. I went on running, or more like staggering, but I finally came upon a small yacht harbor by middle afternoon, and begged a beer and a bed to lie down on. I guess I passed out. They found my name and my phone number in my wallet and went over to Matecumbe and called my wife. She came and got me and took me home. I fell into bed again right away, and slept again like I've never slept for years. I woke up this morning a new man. I've never felt better."

"That was a run for your life, Edward. Now do it every day," said Harry.

Lady Godiva

Ann Carleton is such a real lady, one could never imagine her doing anything unseemly or inappropriate or too risqué. However, she also has a sense of humor and a sense of fun. Besides, that it was all for a good cause: the Waterfront Playhouse was about to begin its new winter season.

As current President of the group, Ann had somehow been persuaded to ride side saddle through town as Lady Godiva, leading a procession of players who were to carry a large sign proclaiming: "Lady Godiva is on her way to buy season tickets to the Waterfront Playhouse.." But fate and fancy decreed all the other participants had mysteriously dematerialized. This left Ann literally saddled with a rented chestnut mare from the upper Keys that couldn't be cancelled. With Johnny DePoo leading the horse, needless to say, she stopped traffic in all directions.

One Key West policeman was heard to report in amazement back at the station: "There's a naked lady riding a horse down Whitehead Street!" When the alerted police car arrived and drove past, the cop shouted, "There she is! There she is!" but then taking stock of the situation: Ann in a full body leotard and wearing a

"Ride on the Wild Side"
Ann Carleton and Johnny DePoo

home made, bright yellow wig that trailed to her ankles, both officers burst into raucous laughter.

Ann Carleton's husband, Guy, was a handsome, neat, crisp, very slim and very ramrod straight British Raj type with a clipped, elegant mustache . He had been titled by their Conch neighbors: "The Duke of Windsor Lane," a very appropriate moniker indeed, since they lived on Windsor Lane. Ann was his lovely Lady. Over the years she became a consummate actress and director of the Water Front Players. Tennessee Williams would often try out his new plays in progress with this talented group to test the waters.

I remember how beautiful she was, as the elegant courtesan "Aunt Alicia" in Gigi, far more beautiful than as Lady Godiva of course. Though I think playing that infamous character was "a ride on the wild side" for Ann that unlocked secret compartments in her psyche that had been undiscovered and lay dormant until then. I'm sure this heroic act broadened her acting range and life considerably. What we do for love.

She will always be remembered as Key West's leading lady of the theater. At the moment she is a young 96 and going strong and as beautiful as ever.

Ann Carleton

Autumn for Mrs. Barnes

It was a marriage of spring and autumn. She was just eighteen and he was almost fifty. His children and his family felt certain that this "pretty young thing" was marrying him for all she could get — his money. I never did know Mrs. Barnes's first name, but I did know that she loved the famous circus man, Alfred Barnes. Actually, she adored him, as a lover, father, companion and friend.

*   *   *

It was late evening, after eleven o'clock, when Opal had closed shop at the Casa Marina and joined Mrs. Barnes, the new owner of the hotel, for a late night supper in her suite. The attractive older woman was restive and unusually talkative. She had had a busy day on the phone with her New York, Chicago, and San Francisco ticket offices. She was owner of the largest theatrical booking agency chain in the country. "I never thought I'd get this far south," Mrs. Barnes laughed. "Another 89 miles and we'd be in Havana listening to Augustine Lara sing 'Solamente Una Vez.' Dear Alfred would have enjoyed that. He loved Latin music."

Opal had had a busy day herself, running between her two attractive gift shops. One she rented in Old Town from my mother — "The Old Island Trading Post" — and the other at the Casa Marina, getting them ready for the winter season. She leaned back and took a sip of her drink, feeling Mrs. Barnes had been kind and flattering to invite her up to relax and have dinner. The two women, both attractive professionals, both of a "certain age" (meaning over forty), had a lot in common. They were hard working, successful widows, though the contrast between Opal's and Mrs. Barnes's success was considerable. Mrs. Barnes was the new owner of the Casa Marina Hotel, that had once been a part of Henry Flagler's sumptuous chain. It was part of his great vision of spanning and linking two continents by railroad, from Canada to the Argentine. The hotel had changed hands several times after World War II, but it was beginning to flourish again, as it had before the War, under Mrs. Barnes's expert touch.

There was a knock at the door and she said, "Enter," and their dinner, Florida lobster, a tomato aspic and champagne on ice, was rolled over to the table where they seated themselves.

"When Alfred died," she said, "I swore I'd never marry again, even if I starved to death. I was so sick of his children's suspiciousness and their rapacious lawyers taking everything. I had no practical or business experience at all, and was totally unworldly, though I knew that I had been taken. So I got a job as a ticket taker at Loew's movie theater on Broadway. It paid for my food, and I had a small estate allowance that covered the rest."

"A month after Alfred died, their lawyer called me. I suppose his conscience had begun to bother him. He said that he had found, in some of the papers, a deed to an orange grove that I had inherited in middle Florida. He said it wasn't worth much, but there was a livable cottage on the land that I could move into or rent out, if I wished."

"It was then that the dreams started. Almost every night I began to dream about my husband. He seemed to be struggling — always toward me, always not quite making it, not being able to communicate. Finally, one night, I had a dream that was so real and vivid that I couldn't deny its message, much less its reality. He was telling me to sell the orange grove. He even went into details about how to sell it, and he said to bank the money and he would tell me what to do next. The day following I called a broker in Florida, and the grove sold almost overnight. Just a few thousand, but a lot more money than I had expected. After that, Alfred appeared in dreams almost every night. We had always been close and loving, but he had been so busy and active in his lifetime, we hadn't had much time to relax together. Now every dream I had about him was a delight and a comfort. I ceased feeling so desperately lonely and abandoned."

"I know you, or anyone hearing this story, will say I unconsciously picked up a lot more from him than I realized while he was alive. But the truth is, I was very young, and not a bit interested in the stock market, or in business generally. And he had managed and handled everything, and provided so generously for me, that I didn't need to think or worry about being practical, or bother about money matters or investment until I had to, after he passed on. Of course, the entertainment world was one that I enjoyed, and Alfred knew a lot about through his marvelous circus, but who would guess I'd end up owning over half the ticket agencies in ten cities, or this lovely hotel. I owe it all to my darling Alfred, who told me exactly what to do and how to invest." She paused. "Now I have almost everything I've ever dreamed of or wanted, except one. A real flesh and blood companion. But Alfred has an answer for that, too. He says I must find one, and that he wants me to be satisfied and fulfilled." She turned and looked almost shyly embarrassed at Opal and confided, "I've had a crush, since I was a girl, on a French entertainer — a singer. We met each other years ago when we were on tour with the circus in Europe. His name is George Trenet, he's Charles Trenet's uncle. He was just beginning to mount the crest of his popularity. Too busy to remember me, I'm sure, but we did meet. I thought he was stunning and charming. And if I hadn't been so happy with Alfred, I would have been smitten. But all that was nearly twenty-five years ago. Do you think he's still alive somewhere?" she asked, turning to Opal, looking almost girlish and uncertain. "Why don't you find out," said Opal with a mischievous smile.

A few days later, Mrs. Barnes hailed Opal in the lobby. "They found him!" she said jubilantly. "He's living in Provence, in Nice — he still has occasional concerts and engagements. His fans are mostly my age, of course, but they say he still has that 'Old Black Magic.' What shall I do? Shall I take a chance and invite him to perform here at the hotel this winter? What do you think?"

"I think it's wonderful," said Opal. "Do it."

Three weeks later, Opal was invited by Mrs. Barnes to join her at the new nightclub of the Casa Marina, called "The Gilded Cage." When she arrived, Opal could see Mrs. Barnes in the company of an attractive older man, elegant and attentive — undoubtedly the featured French singer. They were sitting, leaning towards each other and smiling into each others' eyes. "It's definitely love," thought Opal. "And Alfred is all for it," confided Mrs. Barnes blissfully later. "He doesn't want me to be alone any longer."

The Southernmost Castle

o you know who the dignified old gentleman could be who lives up in the turret somewhere on the third floor?" the attractive young artist Avery Johnson asked Miss Jessie. "I pass him so often coming or going on the stairs. He always nods and smiles at me when we pass but I never run into him anyplace else where we could talk."

"Sometimes I see him when I look out my window. He often stands under the Coconut palm by the sea wall and always around sunset. It must be his favorite place to stand, looking out to sea. His little bulldog is always next to him. The two are quite a sight together!"

Sometime after Florida (Curry) Harris, my great-grandmother Louisa Curry Porter's younger sister and her husband Vining Harris, died, the Southernmost House — their big castle-like home at the top of Duval Street — was sold. For a time, just after WWII, Walter Chrysler, grandson of the founder of Chrysler Motors, who had been stationed in the Navy here during the war, bought it and made it into an attractive restaurant/dinner club.

The Southernmost Castle at the foot of Duval Street
Artist – Arnaud Dalbissin

Before that, when this story takes place, it was an Inn with a lending library downstairs. The two top floors were rented out to paying guests. One of them was my mother's friend, artist Avery Johnson, who lived there for a period of time during the WPA period.

As a child I remember playing in the gardens and up in the turrets with my same-age cousin Barbara, the Harris' granddaughter. We could often hear the voice of Aunt Florida bugling for her husband across the gardens, "VI-I-I-I-I-ning-g-g-g!" Her call floated in the breeze, unfolding streamer-like over the beds of pansies, and petunias and periwinkles, over the hedges of bougainvillea, through the Australian Pines, finally to wrap itself like a long tentacle around the solitary male figure standing under one of the palms at the edge of the seawall. Uncle Vining, hearing it, would turn slowly from this favorite meditation spot as though on an automatic switch and head for the castle-like house and Aunt Florida waiting majestically on the big sea porch for him.

Aunt Florida was a formidable personality as were all the Curry girls. It was often said that unfortunately it was his daughters who had inherited their father William Curry's drive and force, rather than his sons. The "girls" had all married successful husbands and ruled over them with benevolent despotism. Hawks and Eagles of Industry, it seems, rarely produce sons of the same feather. Sons, generally, are much milder and gentler birds than their aggressive patriarchal fathers.

Avery Johnson continued his inquiring conversation with my mother: "The old gentleman is always dressed in beautifully tailored and immaculate white linen," he said, " a white linen suit, white linen shirt, and a light colored bow tie. He carries a very fine, white straw Panama. He has a carefully trimmed white mustache and goatee and very friendly smiling blue eyes. Have you any idea who he could be?" Jessie looked astonished. "Why, Avery," she gasped, "you're describing Vining Harris! You must be seeing his ghost!"

So on soft breezy afternoons, around sunset, when the big piled up pink clouds are floating over the Gulf Stream and over Havana, if you're inclined, walk out on the pier at the end of Duval St. and listen. If you are lucky, you'll hear a clear clarion voice carried on the offshore breeze calling, "VI-I-I-I-I-ning-g-g-!" And sometimes, if you are even luckier, you will see a solitary figure all dressed in white linen standing under a palm by the sea wall. He will turn very slowly and with a small black and white bulldog at his heels, head toward a solitary and commanding figure waiting for him on the porch of the the big sea Castle house on the Southernmost point of the U.S.A.

Night Time – Star Time Key West

Old Key West

The Three Young Lady Daughters
Good Night Irene
Conga Julia
On the Beach
Captain Cole

The Audubon House

Three Young Lady Daughters

It had been rumored that Captain Geiger in his early youth had been a pirate. Nevertheless , like many reformed sinners before and after him, he had met a pretty Key West girl, married her and settled down to become one of the pillars of the community, as well as its harbor pilot during and after Commodore David Porter's tenure here. His wife had died in a yellow fever outbreak leaving him with three daughters. Geiger, knowing the wiles and waywardness of the world, had taken great pains to raise his girls with the strictest and most proper decorum. His home, (now the Audubon House Museum), an elegantly restored sea captain's house on Whitehead Street maintained by the Mitchell Wolfson family, is especially distinguished by its three second-floor cupolas looking out to sea. Therein lies our story.

In the spring of 1850, the U.S. Navy, flexing its muscles as part of a young and growing nation, arrived in Key West waters and anchored in Man O'War Bay. The unofficial object of the visit was to relax from strenuous maneuvers and to enjoy life a bit.

The U.S. Navy anchored in Man-O-War Bay

In those days the Geiger-Audubon House, before the navy yard was filled in and expanded, was located very near the water and the view from its three cupola windows was expansive and commanding. On this occasion, at least twenty-five or thirty vessels could be clearly seen off shore. The fleet had hardly arrived and set anchor when Captain Geiger, who had sent a tender out beforehand to the Admiral to announce his intended visit, had himself rowed out post haste to the flagship. His was a clear mission in mind.

Once aboard he was received ceremoniously and ushered down to the wardroom where he was greeted by the Admiral. Captain Geiger, after the usual civilities, wasted no time in getting to the point of his visit:

"Admiral," he said, "what's this I hear about your men swimming overboard with no clothes on?"

The Admiral's eyebrows raised in surprise: "That's so, Captain Geiger," he responded. "We have been at sea for over thirty days. This is the first opportunity our men have had to relax — have a bath!"

"But," enjoined Captain Geiger, "I'm told there are over two thousand men out here and all naked as jaybirds!"

"That's so," again agreed the Admiral, smiling. "But what difference does it make? We're anchored over a mile and a half out from shore!"

"It does make a difference, Admiral. I assure you, sir," declared Geiger. He paused, then announced. "I have three young lady daughters!"

"But Captain," responded the Admiral, bewildered, "what possible difference could it make to your three young lady daughters if my men are swimming with no clothes on?"

"Admiral!" said Captain Geiger pounding the wardroom table for emphasis, "It does make a difference! Sir, my daughters have spyglasses!"

Goodnight Irene

Prologue

In the 1870's Irene Bethel was know as the most beautiful woman on the island. She reigned as both Queen of the Wreckers and as the elegant costumed Queen of the international chess games held in the black and white tiled grand ballroom of the Cuban Club. Irene met and married handsome, audacious, and adventurous Bradish W. Johnson in the late 70s. The two, destined to love and to battle even through almost unheard of divorce in the 1890's and remarriage, epitomized the dramatic high spirits and drama of Key West's colorful wrecking days.

*   *   *

Miss Irene came floating toward us in the gloom of the La Concha portico looking like a ghost ship adrift on a windless night sea. It was after nine, a hot summer evening, and everybody had been forced out of their steamy houses to catch a breath of fresh air and have ices at Lucignani's on Duval Street.

Dressed in her best white chiffon, she was looking unusually tidy. Her white hair had been neatly combed back from her high, pale forehead into a bun at the nape of her long neck instead of falling around her face in its usual careless wisps. Tall and graceful with high cheekbones and dark-lashed sea blue eyes, she was a Bethel, one of the early wrecking families originally from the Bahamas to settle here.

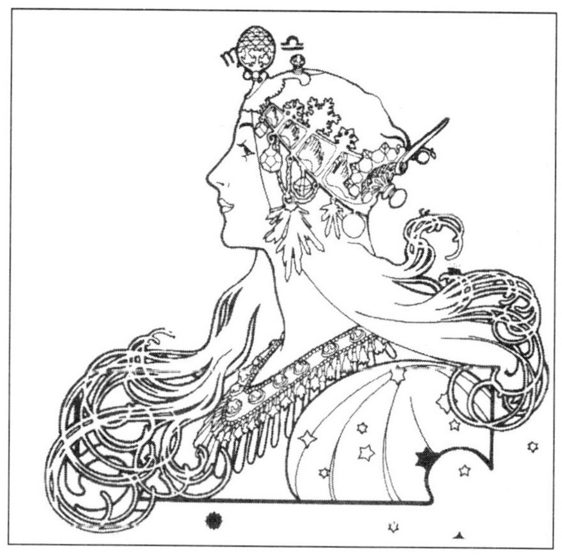

Irene Johnson as Queen of the International Chess Games

Irene had met and married Bradish Johnson, nicknamed 'Hog' by his jealous but admiring peers (Hog always got to the wrecks first). His prominent family had been founders of the New York Yacht Club famed for building the fastest sailing clipper ships of the day. He was an Annapolis graduate who had found the regular Navy too slow-going after the Civil War, bailed out and into seal hunting in Alaska and then filibustering in the Caribbean. Filibustering then was the risky and profitable business of selling arms to both sides in the numerous small Latin American revolutions. His competitive successes had given him his moniker and made him King of the Wreckers by the late 1800's.

My grandfather, Will Porter, then a boy of eleven or twelve, remembers holding Miss Irene's queen train as her page boy for hours at a time. International chess games used beautifully costumed human pawns and pieces, while the audience looked down from the second floor surrounding balconies observing the moves

Braddish W. Johnson c.1860

and strategies of the contending champions.

"I never minded having to stand still for so long," he remembered with pleasure. "The queen hardly ever moved, but I didn't care at all. I could just stand there and look at her. She was very beautiful!"

We stopped abreast and greeted our next door neighbor warmly. "Good evening Miss Irene. Where are you headed?" we asked politely, smiling at our old friend. We felt more than casual interest. Her mind had been adrift and wandering lately, and we were concerned about her. My mother felt that living alone, she was not taking care of herself or eating properly, and looked too thin.

"Going our way?" asked my father, trying to sound light and casual.

Miss Irene's voice still contained a lovely silken quality. It was almost all that was left of her great beauty.

"Heading for the bank," she chimed melodiously, looking at us with pleasure and purpose.

As we stood chatting together my father noticed when she dropped a large white envelope on the sidewalk. He stooped to pick it up. She was unaware that she had dropped it. He pocketed it for safe keeping, to give back to her later.

"It's later than you think, Miss Irene," we told her, trying to make light of her confusion. "The bank has already closed. Why don't you come home with us now? You can go as soon as it opens tomorrow morning." As they said this, Jessie and Wallace amicably linked arms with her while I brought up the rear. We turned her unprotesting toward her home on Whitehead Street and she seemed almost relieved to be captured and escorted home. It was too hot to protest anyway.

A little while later, mother and I were helping to settle her into bed.

Miss Irene was laying back on a prop of paisley pillows piled up high behind her. The room and the house were filled with fascinating sea-faring artifacts from the days when she and Bradish had cruised around the Caribbean on their honeymoon, or treasures that he had salvaged and acquired later as a wrecker. Several mahogany sea chests, whose contents she had already shown me, were full of objects and mementos of her husband's voyages all over the world.

Now lying back and relaxed, she was trying to behave very patiently, allowing Jessie to help her. "Miss Irene," Jessie began hesitantly, patting and plumping up the pillows behind her, "Don't you have anybody who could come live here with you?" she asked, and then continued, gaining courage. "This is such a big house to live in alone and to take care of by yourself." She glanced quickly at scattered belongings in disarray all around the room. "Don't you have some relative who would appreciate living here with you, who could do some shopping and food preparing? Someone to see that you eat properly and keep the house for you?"

Generally very independent and proud, it was plain that Miss Irene was politely tolerating and indulging her neighbor trying to help her. Her eyes were half closed and as she leaned back against the pillows, considering Jessie's question. Then, in her soft, beautifully melodious voice she chimed answer, "I have one sister, and I hate her like hell."

✳   ✳   ✳

Just to be sure my father banked the contents of the envelope in her account the next day. It contained $500 in cash, a lot of money in those Depression days. Miss Irene's sister, whom she "hated like hell," arrived several weeks later. We had gone North by then for the summer when this un-benevolent sister had Miss Irene declared non compos mentis and put her in the old folks home on Poor House Lane. She then proceeded to ransack Miss Irene's house, tearing up floorboards and pulling off wallpaper looking for hidden money, which she undoubtedly found, for she left town quickly after.

Miss Irene died within a few weeks of her confinement, while we were still away. We were desolate, finding out on our return the fate of our beloved neighbor and my favorite storytelling friend. But, it was tragically too late to save her.

I haven't given up looking for the pirate treasure that Miss Irene assured me was buried somewhere in our garden. Could it be near the pirate grave on the west side of the house ?. . . or under the big Spanish lime tree by the side driveway ?. . . perhaps under the old cookhouse patio floor near the chimney ?. . . or could it be near the pirate well? I'll go on wondering all my life.

Heritage House Museum has a number of artifacts that belonged to Bradish and Irene: two mahogany sea chests, one made for Irene for their honeymoon sail around the Caribbean and one that had belonged to her husbands Swedish first mate; Chinese fans and other objects of art also belonged to her. Bradish brought them back as gifts from his salvaging days when they were King and Queen of the Key West Wreckers.

*　　*　　*

EPILOGUE

My parents, Jessie and Wallace Kirke, bought Miss Irene's property after her death, but her house was too far gone with termite damage to be saved or restored, and had to be torn down. Later, my mother bought the Stowers' house, that stood next to the Strand Theater on Duval Street. It was going to be destroyed so she bought it and moved it to the spot where Miss Irene's house had been. It is now part of Kelly's Restaurant. In doing this Miss Jessie continued an old tradition in Key West: dismantling and moving the wooden pegged houses by "sailing" them like ships around the island to new locations.

The Pirate Grave that was sculpted out of coral rock, on our shared property line, tempts me still to believe that pirate or Spanish treasure still lies buried as Miss Irene said, somewhere in this old historic garden. Perhaps my grandson's Kieran and Kyle will finally discover it. But please don't disturb the old Dutch oven, boys!

Wreckers at Work

Conga Julia
Key West's
African Queen

Prologue

When we were living on the great island of Madagascar in the 1970s, there existed ten tribal queens quite alive and thriving there. This ancient system of royalty was matriarchal, with title passing from mother to daughter. I do not believe that Conga Julia had any children, but there are still people living here in Key West, in the older black community, who knew her, and perhaps would remember.

Still, few people realized that Key West has had its very own African Queen, and that her name was Conga Julia (pronounced "Hoolia"). She was, I believe, originally from the Ivory Coast in Africa.

At the very beginning of the Civil War, Conga Julia and perhaps most of her tribe were held captive aboard two British slavers headed for the New World. The slave ships were themselves captured by the Union Navy in Key West waters and the Africans on board, with their young queen, were brought ashore to live in baracoons (make-shift huts) built on the parade field of Fort Taylor. Here they were kept isolated for fear of possible contagion from leprosy, cholera and other fevers, for the duration. At the end of the Civil War, the tribe was released and given the choice of returning to the newly established African homeland, Liberia, or remaining here in the U.S.

British Slave Ship

Conga Julia, along with about thirty percent of her tribe, chose to remain here, and it is this group, never actually sold as slaves, who are the ancestors of many of our proud black families in Key West today.

When I was living in Paris in the middle 60s, I frequently went to the Museum of Man in the Palais de Chaillot. Human physical characteristics and traits were fascinatingly identified and displayed there. A feature I noted and recognized with interest was the prominence of the posterior of the tribal peoples of the Ivory Coast — often so flat at the top of the derierre that one could have balanced a cup and saucer upon it. Except for this same prominence, Conga Julia was very tall and thin, almost emaciated. She was also the island's Voodoo high priestess, very proud and rather severe looking. The Island children generally respected and feared her. When obstreperous and unruly, all their mothers had to do to

African Mask

regain control over them was to mutter threateningly, "If you don't behave yourself, I'll tell Conga Julia on you." That was enough warning to quiet down the noisiest and rowdiest behavior.

Conga Julia lived in a small Conch cottage at the top of Solares Hill that was set back from the street behind a picket fence with herb gardens in the front and rear. The house was a weather-beaten silvery-gray, except for the frames of all the windows and the front door. These were painted a vibrant and luminously electric "Hail Mary Blue," as it was called, a color that was believed to ward off and protect the inhabitants within from evil spirits.

Conga Julia was an impressively knowledgeable herbalist. My great grandfather, Dr. J.Y. Porter, respected and learned much from her expertise. He had planted the borders of his own property with leafy spindly tamarind trees. Their shelled pods could be steeped in hot water and reduced to a tincture that was considered a recuperative tonic for yellow and other fevers.

Conga Julia was both revered as voodoo high priestess and partially feared by most of the island. She reputedly died in the early 40s at the Olympian age of 120, a figure that does not seem realistic or accurate to me. However, she was very old.

She was ceremoniously, but secretly buried with tribal totems and drums. Later, these were dug up and copied by her followers, and then reburied — no outsider knows just where today.

Off Whitehead Street, on Petronia near Thomas, a gigantic Indigo tree still stands. This is in the neighborhood where Conga Julia once reigned. The tree's seasonal clusters of apple green berries spring strangely and directly out of its huge trunk on small lightning-like branches. The tree at this time looks bewitched. Kitty-corner and across from it is an empty lot that was once obscured from Thomas Street by dense high cane grass. There, it was said, voodoo rights were celebrated in its interior. In my youth, before hurricanes when driving up Whitehead Street, this area would pulse and reverberate with the beating sound of African drums heard all over this part of the island. Many believed that their sound vibrations could and would counteract and equalize the drop of barometric pressure happening outside with that inside the human body, and so helped avoid stress and illness. Be that as it may — this area of town where she once reigned still feels permeated and haunted by the proud and powerful spirit of Conga Julia.

Lane in Bahama Village

On the Beach

See that man raking the beach?" Miss Jessie pointed to a deeply tanned, sunscorched, long-haired hippie piling up sea-weed on the city beach at the end of Duval Street. She declared: "He's a direct descendant of Louis XIV."

I looked at my mother skeptically and then back at the raker on the beach and felt Miss Jessie's sense of the absurd had gone too far. Louis XIV, indeed! But, at that moment the beach cleaner turned his head toward us and then back to profile and I caught my breath. First the flash of very blue Bourbon eyes, and then, there it was; in all its glory, the Bourbon Nose! I couldn't believe my eyes. How could this be possible?

"Oh, but, it is," said my mother.

I had just returned for a visit home from Paris where I was currently living with my family near Versailles. The growth and cultivation of the Bourbon nose was an historic event well documented in that region. All the Louis came into the world with short pug noses and gradually, like pedigreed dachshunds, grew them to full splendour by age thirty-five or forty. Here it was on the Key West beach raking seaweed at the thirty-five year stage!

I turned to my mother and asked incredulously, "How did it get here?"

"With great difficulty," laughed Miss Jessie and then began to tell this story.

When the French Revolution broke out, all the aristocrats and nobility tried to escape with their lives. One of Louis XV's many mistresses had been a beautiful titled girl from Martinique. Her son by the king, as was the custom with all the royal bastards, had been well educated — this one as a doctor of medicine. When his mother, now an older aristocrat, was guillotined, he fled France by ship,

Louis XIV of France

and headed for her island of Martinique, hoping to find safe haven there.

Fate still dealt him yet another blow, for his ship was attacked on the high seas and captured by pirates.

As was often the case in piratical waters, all the other passengers aboard were made to walk the plank so that they could not live to testify as witnesses. Philippe, however, was discovered at the last moment to be a doctor.

It so happened that the ship's crew was rife with scurvy and the pirate captain, learning of his medical training, drew him aside and asked if he could help with the dreaded illness. Philippe, of course, said he could and did, and so became such a favorite with the crew that they invited him to join and become one of them.

I looked out to the sinewy beachcomber and thought about Philippe whose past was being destroyed and whose future was very uncertain. What could he lose? The pirate chieftain, realizing Philippe's potential and advantages as a physician and gentleman aristocrat, set him up in Key West as a front to dispose of their captured booty.

As befitting a physician, Philippe settled into a handsome sea carpenter house on lower Elizabeth Street near Caroline. Caroline Street at that time and place, before the land was filled in, was conveniently on the water where the loot could be brought in at night. He married a Key West girl, practiced medicine, and on the side was a discreet and expert agent and liaison for the pirates in transporting and disposing of their plunder to markets in New Orleans and Charleston.

Miss Jessie finished with a smile, "So there you see one of Louis XIV's direct descendants."

"What a story!" I marveled, looking out at the beachcomber. "The likes of Louis XIV raking sea-weed on a Key West Beach!"

Captain Cole
The Man Who
Wouldn't Be King

he Oldest House (The Wrecker's Museum) on Duval Street was the home of Captain Watlington and his family. I remember, as a little girl, visiting the two spinster sisters, Miss Lillie and Miss Hannah, who were always kind to me as a child, showing me fascinating objects including a portrait done by Audubon of their father, Captain Watlington, and giving me delicious fresh limeade to drink. But there was also another name: Captain Cole, who had lived in that house as well. His great-granddaughter, a woman my age, came to see me several years ago and told me this delightful story.

She said the name Cole, like the nursery rhyme "Old King Cole," was really an adaptation of the Norwegian name Kohl — that "Old King Cole" was probably a Viking chieftain who had come into England from Norway. Anyway, Captain Cole's granddaughter said that in the late 1800s when her great grandfather was

The Oldest House - The Wreckers House by Wallace Kirke – 1950s

alive and living in the Oldest House, a contingent from Norway arrived and anchored in the harbor.

It seems that their country was fresh out of kings and they had been sent officially to find Captain Cole, who was really Captain Kohl, and a direct descendant in line for the crown of Norway. They had come to invite him to return with them to become their king.

Her story goes that the captain invited them all to a sumptuous dinner at his home. During it, they toasted, Scandinavian style, almost everything as well as each other and then he thanked them most graciously for the honor they would bestow on him. But, "thank you very much, gentlemen," and "with all due respect," he preferred, he admitted, to remain here and go on living in Key West.

Old Family Stories

Surrender
William Curry
Saving Grace

Dr. Joseph Yates Porter – c.1910

Surrender

Prologue - Dr. J.Y. Porter

Doctor Joseph Yates Porter was Florida's first State Board of Health Director from 1889-1917, covering the period before the Spanish-American War and after World War I. He became a pioneer in preventative medicine (then called sanitation) and in controlling contagions. Dr. Porter is credited with being the primary force in wiping out the dreaded yellow fever. Today his systems and methods, particularly in the area of spread and control of contagion and systems of sanitation, have become not only accepted and used nationally, but internationally as well. His regulation requiring a health officer to board and examine every ship arriving in port from a foreign country before passengers and crew are allowed to disembark, is now an international procedure

Dr. Porter's advice to his friend Henry Flagler, that communal drinking glasses then used aboard the Florida East Coast Railroad should be prohibited and replaced by the prototype for "Dixie Cups," the first disposable paper drinking vessels, which were originally used on Flagler's trains.

An interesting anecdote about Dr. Porter and his long and dedicated career in Florida, occurred when the smallpox vaccine first became available to the public. As Public Health Officer in charge he requested that all citizens in Key West be inoculated. Many very independent Conchs refused. After repeated patient requests, the good Doctor saw fit to quarantine the entire island. No one could come in or leave until they were inoculated. The mavericks finally gave in, but with much protest. However, Dr. Porter was highly appreciated by them for this effort later on.

Grandfather Porter writes in his medical memoir, *Millstones and Milestones: Looking Backward Over Fifty Years of Health Work in Florida* (it is as applicable today as it was more than one hundred years ago): "In the summer of 1867, while studying medicine in the office of an ex-Army Surgeon, Dr. Wm. G. Cornick, the writer contracted yellow fever during an epidemic which prevailed in the city of Key West that year. A recital of my case would be interesting to medical men for two reasons: First, the amount of ignorant medication the human system can stand and throw off — for I was desperately ill; second, the fact that no one dies until his or her predestined time arrives."

It is this far-reaching and far seeing view that hallmarks the prophetic career of this fine physician.

*　　*　　*

SURRENDER

When the Civil War broke out, Grandfather Porter was just a boy of fourteen. He and his grandmother, Susan Browne Randolph (sister of prominent lawyer and business man Fielding Browne, whose son Jefferson Browne later wrote the history of Key West) were left in the big family home — The Webb Porter House on the

Dr. J.Y. Porter with his grandchildren c.1906 left to right: Minnie Porter Harris; baby Wm Curry Harris, Joe Porter Mountjoy & Jessie Louise porter

corner of Caroline and Duval Streets. The two alone had survived the death of all the other members of the family from yellow fever.

Joseph was a handsome, blond boy and a leader, even then, among his peers. He had developed a determination and inner strength gained through the loss of his mother, Anne Randolph Porter, when he was twelve and his father, Joseph Yates Porter, even before his birth. His maternal grandfather, Captain Thomas Mann Randolph, originally from Virginia, had been in command of the Revenue Service that would later be called the U. S. Coast Guard. It had replaced Commodore Porter's anti-piratical fleet in the Caribbean. Tragically, Captain Randolph, too, had died in a yellow fever outbreak, leaving Joseph and his grandmother, Susan, in each other's care.

At the outbreak of the Civil War, the Island's greatest sympathy was with the Confederacy, though many Key Westers, including Susan Randolph, had friends and relatives living in the North.

The day before, to the dismay of the Island, Major French, then commander of the militia stationed at the army barracks on White Street, had made a surprise march from the garrison across the island to occupy and claim Fort Taylor in the name of the Union. This put the fort in Northern hands for the duration of the war. It was a most strategic move since it secured Key West as the base for the Union navy blockading the Gulf ports and cut off the South from European sympathizers and supplies, thus helping to strongly influence the outcome of the war in favor of the North.

The Islanders all knew Commander French and were grateful and indebted to him. It was he who had personally prevented the transport of many Key West citizens as Southern sympathizers to detention centers in the North. Had it not been for him, many Key Westers would have been confined and exiled from the Island for the duration of the war.

Young Joseph woke up this early morning bursting with patriotic fury and determination to recapture the fort for the South.

Being the sole remaining man of his family, he rounded up a group of his peers, a dozen or more boys all in their early teens. They set out, a gallant but undisciplined host, clutching their fathers' swords or whatever weapons they could find, and proceeded to march bravely out the long causeway over the water leading to Fort Taylor.

The breeze blew in from the sea fanning their perspiring brows as they marched in the hot sun. In the distance the fort loomed up ominously in front of them, growing more and more massive with every step. (It was much larger at that time than it is today. The original top tier was later removed to make it less of a target from the sea.) Meanwhile, the boys' approach had been noted by the guard on duty on the ramparts, and Major French had been summoned. He arrived simultaneously with the young troops, who halted and stood looking belligerently but with uncertainty at the huge closed gate entrance. Joseph, as their leader, drew himself up to his fullest adolescent height and stepped forward. Brandishing his grandfather's sword, he looked up at the now visible Major and fiercely demanded in his loudest and deepest voice the surrender of the fort in the name of the Confederacy.

Commander French, from the rampart looking down on the perspiring and resolute boys, recognized most of them as members of families he knew on the Island. He knit his brows and looked as stern and severe as possible back at them and bellowed: "IF YOU DON'T GO HOME THIS MINUTE, I'M COMING DOWN THERE TO TAKE THE FLAT OF MY SWORD TO THE FLAT OF YOUR BOTTOMS!"

This unexpected command was received and followed by a profound silence. Slowly a terrible eternal minute passed. Then, without a word, Joseph lowered his grandfather's sword and the young troop turned on their heels. With bowed heads and drooping shoulders they began the slow, humiliating march back down the long, long causeway towards manhood.

In later years, Grandfather Porter confessed that in his entire life, he never experienced, ever again, so ignominious and devastating a defeat.

*   *   *

"The Everglades are Florida's natural airconditioning system declared Dr. Porter. If we drain them," he warned, "Florida will become hotter in the summer and cooler in the winter. It will alter and change the climate of the entire state."

Ft. Taylor and the long causeway - 1860
All the land on either side of the long causeway was later filled in during the
successive wars – becoming now part of Fort Taylor National Park.

Full Moon in Key West – The Dudleys

William Curry

reat-Great grandfather William Curry must have had a very active and prophetic sixth sense. How he knew what the New York and world stock markets were doing from far flung Key West is still a mystery. However, he invested with enormous success, becoming Florida's first million-aire, and owner of the largest ships' chandlery in all the South and Gulf region.

Something definite, however, can be gleaned from his affluence about the scope of world-connected trade that Key West enjoyed and was privy to during the height of its wrecking period (1820s - 1860). It was this period that produced the island's finest architec-ture, the Caribbean colonial style, and established the unique and varied look of Old Town. These houses were so well-built and last-ing that the deep economic trough that followed the decline of wrecking did not destroy them, nor the Key Westers that hung on to life here to ride out the later, even deeper, economic depressions. These sea carpenter houses could be considered among the world's first "Pre-fabs" since they were put together with tongue-in-groove construction and held together with wooden pegs so that they

Bond belonging to and signed by William Curry

could be dismantled and moved around.

William Curry's huge and imposing ships' chandlery stood on the water on the northwest side of the island, where the Hyatt Hotel and The Galleon are today. In the old days, from Curry Sons towers and turrets flew flags of welcome to visitors from all the world over. On its porches and galleries the wives, families and friends of expected voyagers returning home would wait to catch a first glimpse and to celebrate their arrival.

My great-grandmother, Louisa Curry, who had married Dr. Joseph Yates Porter, was William Curry's oldest daughter. This short and insightful story comes down from her.

*   *   *

The Curry family, originally from Scotland, had settled in the Carolinas in the mid-1700s and had become successful landowners and planters. However, they remained loyalists when the Revolutionary War broke out and were forced to flee to the British-held Bahamas. William Curry, born at Cat Key in the early 1800s, arrived in Key West at age 15 to make his fortune, which indeed he did. Starting on the lowest rung of the ladder, he worked for Wall and Baldwin, successful business men in merchandising and was paid the handsome sum of four dollars a week. This amount barely covered food

William Curry, 1870s

and lodging in a tiny room with a few cents left over for clothes and entertainment. On his way to work each day to the offices of Wall & Co., Curry passed a window displaying ships' fittings and supplies. In view as part of the collection was a beautiful, small hand compass that caught his fancy. He began to yearn for it, finally saving enough money over many weeks to buy it. Triumphantly, he brought it back to his small quarters and hung it on a wall to admire. It hung there day after day, unchanging and inactive. Finally, in disgust with himself, he tore the compass off the wall and ran down to the end of the nearest dock and threw it as far as he could out into the water. Vowing that he would never again buy another thing that just looked beautiful but was not currently useful.

This is the background of the famous, sumptuous solid gold tea and dinner service that he later purchased from Tiffany's in New York. It fulfilled the requirement of his lesson and vow:

My grandfather, William R. Porter, William Curry's oldest grandson, inherited the carving set from this collection and it is now on display in the Heritage House Museum.

Curry Sons – Just before its destruction by fire.

The Saving Grace

Uncle Billy and his favorite nephew, young J.Y. Porter IV, were sitting amicably together in big rockers on William Porter's front porch waiting to be called in for dinner. J.Y.'s feet and legs encased in braces from polio could still not quite touch the ground. As was his need and habit, the youngest member of the family enjoyed talking and confiding in his uncle, the oldest son of the illustrious Dr. Porter and his wife Louisa.

"I just don't see what Grandfather Porter saw in Grandmother Louisa," said J.Y. "She was such an unpleasant person." J.Y. often sought his uncle Billy's opinion on various subjects and he continued: "Grandfather was such a wonderful man. He did so much for so many people. For the life of me I can't see what he ever saw in Grandma Louisa. I don't think she had anything at all to recommend her - not one thing!" he said with conviction.

His uncle caught by surprise by this unexpected confession about his mother drew himself up indignantly. "No such a thing, son," he replied with emotion. "She played the piano beautifully!!"

Jessie & cousin John Henry Newton in Venice – 1924

Miss Jessie

Miss Jessie Speaks
Ginseng
All First Prizes
Miss Jessie and Age
Forgetting
Better to Chew With
Presidential Cracks

Miss Jessie

Miss Jessie Speaks
as told to Bill Lorraine

When I was ten years old I was blinded for three weeks. I was playing in the sand at Atlantic City and somebody poked me in the eye with an umbrella. They took me to a doctor at the Delaware Water Gap and I had to wear a covering over both eyes. It was terrible at the time, but it did something wonderful for me. I can see the Delaware Water Gap now, with the sky and the trees and gradations of color as they were then, when they first took off my bandages. I saw color for the first time. It brushed past me, as it does the poet. I forgot about the incident as a child but it came back to me in my subconscious, and later I knew it expanded my appreciation of things.

We have within us all our emotional responses to the world outside, it's in our adrenaline, and we must hit out against injustice when we see it. We must do! Act! Not watch T.V. We have become a nation of escapists, not a nation of seekers. It's rare to find a seeker. And the difference is in the art of conversation. T.V.

saves people the trouble of thinking and has changed this country into a place where people don't talk to one another. And what you don't use, you lose. Stimulating conversation used to be the evening's entertainment when I was a young girl. And conversation around the table at meal time is how I learned much of what I know today. Dinner at our house was an event. The young children ate in the pantry with the nurse. The house

Jessie Porter 1920

was big, there was plenty of help, and house guests were the order of the day. My mother made one rule I am very thankful for. I had to have something interesting to offer in the way of conversation before I could come to the dinner table with the grown folks. You stay with the things you learn as a child. Now, I like to dine, even if it's on a graham cracker, and while dining, I like to talk about the things we learned today, the things that have made us think.

The Depression in Key West wasn't like it was in New York City, where there was no dirt to grow food in and the people got frightened. My father, who was the banker with the responsibility of the town weighing heavily on him with the only bank in town that didn't fold, was persuaded by my mother to start growing fruits at the other end of the Island. He had planted a lime and veg-table grove in the Poinciana area that raised okra, tomatoes, watermelons, cantaloupes, and banana melons, which were rough-skinned melon about two feet long and were delicious. He watched the slow process of the seeds he had planted changing into fruit, and it saved his sanity

*   *   *

The vocation of every Southern woman was to make herself atractive to men. She'd live through her men. She was taught always to know enough to appreciate, but not enough to contradict her man. I dislike the old South from the woman's point of view. It was cruel: if she wasn't attractive, she was helpless. Women who didn't marry were old maids, and there was no place in society for them. In a way, women of the old South were in slavery too. When you become dependent on someone to serve your physical needs, you forget how to do it yourself. You forget how.

But they first real slaves from Africa were taken to New England and the found that they couldn't live in the cold climate, so New England developed another type of slavery called indentured servants. They were white workers from Europe who signed up to serve their masters and once indentured they couldn't move away. In 1828, a law was passed forbidding any more importation of slaves to the United States, and Thomas Mann Randolph from Virginia, a great grandfather of mine, was sent to Key West to command the Revenue Cutter Service, the predecessor of the Coast Guard. He came here to bottle-up the entrance to the Gulf of Mexico because slave running was biggest in Louisiana and the Old South. Randolph caught many slaveships here and the enslaved passengers often had diseases — smallpox, cholera, even the plague. So baracoons were set up for quarantine on the southern shore of the Island, where the Navy station is now. And once they were declared free of diseases, the slaves were freed at the bara-coons, and many in time became valuable citizens of the Island.

Too many people have no roots today. And we need to learn about our heritage so we can know of our possibilities. That may be why so many young people come to me, looking for something that assures them of a continuity between the past and the future.

Jessie Porter 1925

Ginseng
as told by Jessie Porter Newton

Dinner at my parents' dinner table was not just dinner. It was an event! Always interesting people were invited — often famous visitors like Gorgas and Goethal on their way to Washington up from building the Panama Canal staying with Grandfather Porter. Or Eldridge Johnson, the man who turned the Victor Talking Machine into an art medium by having Caruso sing for it. For years Henry Flagler came and stayed with us when he was building his Overseas Railroad down the Florida Keys to Key West. He was such a delightful man. I remember sitting at his feet as a little girl in my child's rocking chair enthralled, listening to him tell what he was doing and planning for Florida. Flagler really set the tone and created what most people think of as Florida today . . . a leisure paradise. It is interesting, too, that Florida would have become the original "Hollywood" film capital, if it hadn't been for one deterrent: The mosquito. It had a wonderful climate with brilliant sunlight for filming, but, alas, it also had mosquitoes, noseeums and sand flies that drove outdoor movie crews mad.

Flagler's visions were monumental, and most of them became realized, except his biggest dream of all: to connect the continents via Cuba and Yucatan and span the North and South American continents with train ferries and railroads.

When I was invited to join the adults for dinner, my mother always insisted that I come looking neat and clean to the dinner table. She would say, "Sophie has been preparing a lovely dinner all day; Annette has set the table with fresh linen, the silver and crystal has been all polished, and she has

Miss Jessie at age eight

showered and changed into a fresh uniform." So I was asked to live up to the occasion too, with my hair neatly brushed and hands and face, along with the rest of me, bathed. Mother also made another rule, one that I will always be grateful to her for making: and that was that I always bring with me some interesting bit of information or a thought or idea to be shared with the other dinner guests at the table. I would usually bone up and read to do this beforehand.

One evening when I was about eight years old and my mother considered it appropriate timing to draw me into the adult conversation, she turned to me and said, "Well, Jessie, tell us what you learned today that is interesting to share with everyone."

I was ready.

"Does anyone know what the first thing was that the colonies had to trade with China after they won their independence from England, after the Revolutionary War?" I asked. "What did we have to sell? Does anybody know?" It had to be something that grew, since we had not yet learned how to manufacture anything, and had bought most everything from England up to then.

Several of the dinner guests were listening, and responded politely, "Tobacco?"

"No, that was too early."

"Corn?"

"No," I said, "that still belonged to the Indians."

"Cotton? Indigo?"

"You'll never guess, so I'll tell you," I said, pleased with myself for baffling the grownups. "It was GINSENG!"

"What do they use Ginseng for?" chimed an Admiral's lady.

To which I confidently replied, "It's an aphrodisiac," and, from my eight year old vantage-point continued, "It makes men strong, and it makes people feel happy."

My mother, instead of saying, "An Aphrodisiac??!!" shocked, simply said, "now isn't that interesting, how did you learn that?"

I said, "The teacher told me, and she had to tell me how to pronounce it. It makes old men feel stronger, and it gives them more life." I continued,: "Ginseng grew wild in shady wet places in the Hudson River Valley. They are roots that look like a lot of carrots joined together, quite like little men. The arms sprouted out and there were two legs branching out with a little knobby body and head, with tiny roots sprouting out like hair. They called it the Mandrake root because of this."

Well, I had the table . . . captivated. Conversation had stopped dead to listen to what was coming "out of the mouths of babes." All adult eyes were riveted on me. It was a glorious feeling. For the first time in my life, I had everyone in the whole adult world in the hollow of my hand.

"I've read all about it," I continued. "We sold it, especially to China, where it was worth it's weight in gold. We traded it for China dishes and rice and silks and tea and other things we needed in exchange."

I felt great satisfaction and the sense of mission accomplished while grown-up eyes met and exchanged looks of wonder. "Thank you, Jessie," my mother said, touching my hand. "That was very interesting." She turned matter-of-factly back to her guests. "Now, Admiral, what were you saying about the China trade?"

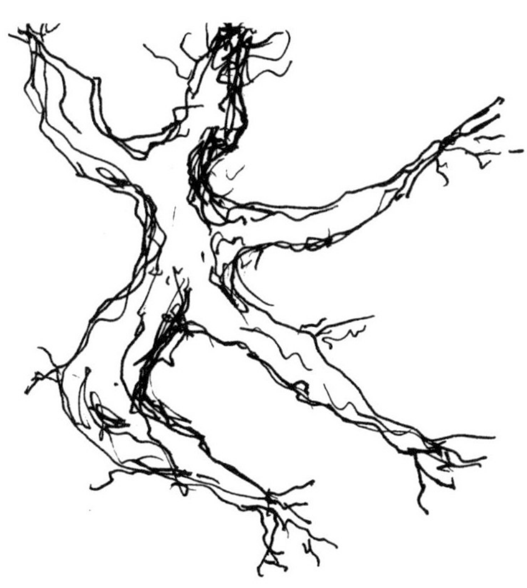

Mandrake Root – Ginsing

All First Prizes

S ince Key West is the only frost-free city in continental U.S.A., many trees and plants flourish here that are unique and not seen in any other part of North America. Our beautiful flower show, held each spring in the scenic old West Martello fort, now named the Joe Allen Garden Center, reflects this diversity. The shows are now tied in with the National Garden Club's rules and regulations. Lovely as they are, especially the fascinating orchid displays, I sometimes wish that we could go back to being our own outlandish selves again.

Miss Jessie organized the first flower show in the mid-30s. It was staged in the Navy yard in one of the longer brick and cement World War I warehouses that was perfect for the show.

Everybody brought their pet potted plants and made flower arrangements from their own gardens. My father, Wallace Kirke, Jessie's first husband, organized the display areas and brought in palms, crotons and hibiscus in large containers to create banks of verdure and color. It was lovely, original and individualistic with

a "to each his own" and "I did it my way" look, i.e. very "Key West-ish." Jessie's selection of judges was unique, too. She chose Ernest Hemingway, John Dos Passos and George Allen England, a writer/adventurer. She also set out a large bowl of well-spiked rum and fruit punch that everybody could enjoy and did — especially the judges. So much so in fact, that they gave everybody in the show first prizes until they ran out of blue ribbons!

*　　　*　　　*

Most of Key West's flowering trees and shrubs were brought here by merchant sea captains (who later settled here) as gifts for their wives. However, the Poinciana, originally from Madagascar, was broadcast by the British all over the Indian, Pacific, and Southern Atlantic oceans to distinguish British-held islands during the summer months. When piracy was especially rife their show of brilliant royal red blossoms could be seen far out at sea signaling a safe harbor rather than a possible pirate nest or enemy stronghold.

*   *   *

Word should be mentioned here about the Fish Fuddle tree that grows indigenously on the Keys. Branches of it would be cut by the Key Indians and thrown into the tide water salt ponds to anesthesise fish. The sap contained a strong anesthetic that put fish into suspended animation where they could be picked out of the water by hand and transferred sometimes for several hours, to another salt water pool ~ quite alive!

Joe Allen Garden – West Martello Towers Flower Show

Tropical Foliage in Key West – The Dudleys

Miss Jessie and Age

Miss Jessie never gave out her age — never. I don't even think she knew it herself. She said age puts labels and limits on what we are. It was only when she died that the Key West Citizen, on its front page, announced it in her obituary. If she had read that, it would have really killed her.

One young newspaper man, whom she had completely charmed after they had talked for a while, asked her hesitantly, "Miss Jessie, do you mind if I ask you a personal question?"

Mother hesitated considering, and then, liking him, said, "Try me."

He asked, "Do you mind telling me how old you are?"

She leaned forward, looking into his eyes, and asked confidentially, "Can you keep a secret?"

"Yes, yes," he responded enthusiastically.

"So can I," said mother.

*   *   *

The State Department has an unexpected sense of humor at

Jesse Porter Newton – 1970

times. Mother and Newt, newly married, were planning to take a trip to Europe. Jessie was about three years older than her new husband, and didn't want this fact to be in black and white or recorded officially anywhere. So when she filled out the passport application papers, where they required the date of birth, she left it blank. Below, on another paper she wrote to them that her great-great-great-great-grandparents had all been born in the U.S. for six or seven generations before the American Revolution, and that it was none of their business what her age was. She must have couched this response with wit. A week or two passed and an answer came from a State Department official saying, "Dear Mrs. Newton. We found your 1920 passport. Ha, ha. We know how old you are!"

Forgetting

Mother was driving me out to the Key West Airport to catch the plane back to Berkeley in California where I was in college. I was showing off my new sophmoric wisdom gleaned partially from a sociology class that included ideas from Hooten's book, *Up From the Ape*.

"The thing that distinguishes man from the lower animals," I informed my mother grandly with all the sweeping perspective of youth, "is his ability to remember."

"Ah", said Mother, responding unhesitantly. "But what makes him human, is his ability to forget!"

The Better to Chew With

Mother looked at the young smiling assistant to a posh Coconut Grove dentist in disbelief. On his desk facing us was a plaster of-Paris replica of her teeth and jaw, reconstructed and also grinning toward us. "Five thousand dollars!" Mother repeated in disbelief, (that would be easily over $25,000 today), "To correct my bite!?!?"

The smile began to fade from the face of the young dentist standing before us, thought, the grinning cast on his desk remained resolutely amused.

Breakfast in the Heritage House garden

"Young man," she continued with conviction, "I've been biting off more than I can chew all my life, I'm not going to put that amount of money into my mouth at my age! I'd put it into my grandchildren's education, but certainly not into my bite!"

The dental fee dropped, with various reasons and rationale below $2,000 some minutes later.

City Beach Key West - foot of Duval street by Wallace Kirke
Old Southernmost House

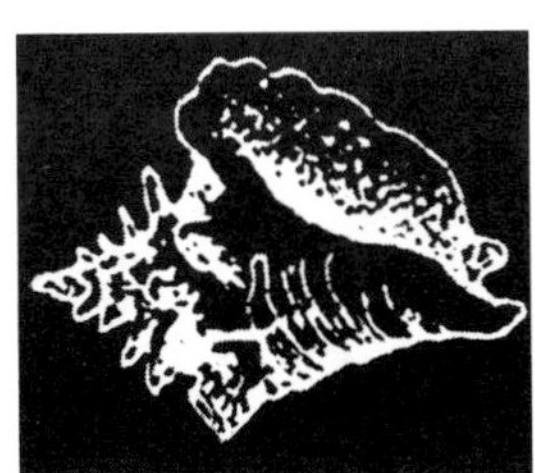

Presidential Cracks

Miss Jessie was a past master at turning lemons into Key Lime pie. 410's (Heritage House) living room ceiling has a series of cracks that, like the spots in the Edgar Allen Poe story, just won't go away. No matter how often we have tried to replaster and eradicate them, they reappear. When bringing in visitors to show how preservation and restoration could transform an old, once neglected classic sea captain house, Mother would wave skyward to the group and ask, "Do you see those cracks?" Everyone would look up to the ceiling at the fault lines that looked like drifting continental plates and she would continue: "Visitors to Key West today often think that Truman was the only president to visit Key West, but of course this isn't so at all. We have had many presidential visitors, including Jefferson Davis after the Civil War, Ulysses S. Grant on his world tour, Teddy Roosevelt, Taft, F.D.R., Eisenhower, Kennedy." Here she would pause.

"When presidents arrive on the island, it was always customary to fire off a twenty-four gun salute from the navy yard nearby to welcome and honor them. These cannon explosions always took their toll in Old Town, breaking window glass and cracking our ceilings. So, ladies and gentlemen," she would add with a pretended smug satisfaction,"we call these our 'Presidential Cracks'." Everyone would look up and regard them with solemn respect and awe, and Miss Jessie would sail on from there.

Heritage House – dining room with Gene Otto painting

Family Helpers

Mammy
Sophie
Hurricane!
Human Hottenin'

Mammy with Grace Dorgan – c.1880

Mammy

Mammy was not only a force to be recognized with in the Campbell-Dorgan-Porter household, she was also one to be listened to with love and respect. For three generations now, she had been an integral part and a mainstay in the family, helping to bring together the Campbell and the Dorgan children into the world as midwife and confidant. "Well, Mammy, we won't be alone now in the New World," the valiant Jean Campbell from Aberdeen, Scotland, had always said triumphantly after each baby was born with Mammy's help.

She had first appeared on Jean's doorstep, a very young black girl barely in her teens, just after the Civil War had ended. She had been "used," as well as beaten and bruised by marauding Union soldiers withdrawing from the New Orleans and Mobile area. Jean took her in and nursed her back to health, and she had stayed on to become part of the family for over forty years.

Here she was now, sitting opposite and looking candidly at her newest charge, whose mother, Grace, she had helped to bring into the world. Jessie was certainly not much to look at. Mobile friends who knew her mother clicked their tongues in sympathy. "My, my, is that

Jessie Porter with Grandmother
Jessie Dorgan and cousin Una 1910

Grace Dorgan's daughter?" they would ask each other in disbelief . "Her mother was such a beauty!"

In a Victorian world that prized looks as a main asset and prime card to play as a woman in the precarious and uneven game of life, they knew Jessie was at a distinct disadvantage. She was not ugly, but at this age she was definitely a plain-looking child with straight fine hair, spindly legs, and high energy that never seemed to tire. Grace would explain to her mother, when little Jessie made her grandmother nervous with her constant activity, "She's just going through one of those difficult stages." After this excuse was repeated over a number of visits, Jessie's grandmother had laughed and commented, "It seems as though little Jessie is just going through one difficult stage after another!"

Now Mammy took Jessie's hand and looked into her eyes. They were sitting together out on the back porch of the big Mobile family home. "I wants to tell you something, Missy, something you should know." Mammy took a deep breath and then began. "Some girls can just sit back and look pretty, and that's all they has to do. And the boys is happy just to come around to look at them." She squeezed Jessie's hand lovingly. "But you can't do that," she said. "You got to learn to talk. And when you talks,"she paused for emphasis and pressed her hand again warmly, "you got to *say* something."

This valuable advice became a cornerstone of Jessie's philosophy all her life.

Sophie

In her entire life, Sophie Brown, my grandparents' wonderful cook, had never been off the Island, not even for a trip up the Keys. She had started off as maid in the Porter household as a very young girl when the older cook had died in harness and she had been trained by my grandmother, Grace Porter. Over the years, most of her culinary secrets, particularly the international ones, she had learned in tandem with my grandmother. Both of them had taste buds as sensitive and subtle as a wine taster's palate. Big Mama would return home from business mixed with pleasure trips to New Orleans, Charleston or New York, with her husband Will Porter, and would head straight for Sophie's kitchen with a packet of written recipes for Sophie to experiment with and learn to cook.

"Here's how I think they created 'such and such a dish' Sophie," she would begin to explain. They would discuss it and then order all the ingredients from Fausto's and Eignhorn's Grocery and Lowe's Fish Market. Sophie would then disappear into her planetary kitchen, emerging several hours later with a

Sophie Brown - master chef for the Porter household for 50 years
taken at Jeane's wedding

steaming dish that Grace would sample and appraise. "Perfect!" Or she would say, "Almost right, but it needs some (more or less whatever)" and Sophie would return to her kitchen to try again.

It was in this way that Sophie became one of the great cooks of the Caribbean. Her realm of Empire and Magic was a big, airy kitchen with a huge black gas range that looked as powerful as a locomotive engine and just as impressive. Sophie's skin was as black and warm as the stove, and so dark that all surrounding light was drawn into it and reflected back as a warm, soft glow of moist radiance.

Jeane and Grace in front of the Woman's club

She stood with legs slightly apart angled like a young colt for balance or like the captain of a sailing ship at his wheel in full command in high seas. Her mantra, her music, was soft, feathery hymns that she hummed all day long and that were barely audible above her breathing. While on duty Sophie never removed her status symbol: a black straw hat that resembled a crushed top hat or some exotic bird's nest. Her eyes were tilted slightly upward with low upper lids shading a perpetual glint of amusement. Her nose was a rollercoaster ending above a wide, generous mouth that also tilted up at the corners and was held there by high cheek bones.

She was an African Queen who somehow, and with great dignity and intention, had arrived and become for over fifty years the cook for the Porter household.

"Would you mind if I asked your cook how she prepared such and such a dish?" dinner guests would often ask Grace, who would always agree and say, "Certainly, go right ahead."

The guest would then, as on safari, searching for lost treasures of Ophir, proceed back through the big, rambling Victorian house, through and past two pantries, past the latticed screened "safes" (small cabinets where fruit and vegetables were stored to ripen), and finally find Sophie at her station, sometimes relaxing with her pipe while Annette the maid cleaned up the dinner dishes.

"Sophie," the enthusiastic guest would declare with pleasure "the . . . was superb! Would you mind telling me how you made it?"

Sophie's face would brighten and glow with a mischievous smile as she prepared to divulge her secrets to the eager guest.

"Well," she would purr in her low, musical voice, "I just takes a handful of fatolean pork, I cuts it up fine, and I puts it in a big pan. Then I takes a handful of chopped onions and I puts them in to fry." As she talked she would move and cup her hand showing imaginary amounts. The inquirer would write down: "handful of fatolean (fat and lean) pork, handful of onions . . ."

"Then I waits and adds coconut milk and a pinch of cumin and a squedge of lemon . . . . " Sophie would continue carefully and pensively.

The guest by this time is showing signs of distress and uncertainty.

"Then I takes a handful of flour sifted and puts that in – slowly."

"Just a minute, please, Sophie," interrupts the acolyte, "how much onion, fatolean pork, flour and so forth and so on?"

Sophie would tilt her head to the side, squint her eyes and consider carefully, then say with feeling and in a warning voice, "Oh, not too much!" and then with conviction and assurance, "jess enuff".

This advice became a favorite family recipe for living: "Not too much — jess enuff."

Hurricane '35

My grandparents' wonderful cook Sophie Brown, thought of the mainland as being just as far away as China. In all her life she never left the island. One of her grandsons, Regis, worked as a handyman for the attractive young couple who owned the Long Key Fishing Lodge. He was the first of her large family to get a job off the Island: "way up there" near Matecumbe Key.

When the 1935 hurricane struck the Middle Keys, first reports came back to Key West that it had taken almost all the inhabitants living there out to sea on a fifteen-foot tidal wave. Regis, along with the lodge couple, the CCC workers, the beautiful Grooms girl and many others were tragically lost, and the railroad was washed out as well. It was a terrible and devastating storm that left Key West in deep despair and depression but almost unscathed physically.

Word began filtering down about the enormity of the damage and loss of life. My grandfather sent Albert Atwell, his boatman, up with his cabin cruiser carrying water and supplies, as did most Key West boat owners. We waited, praying to hear of survivors.

Photo is from Ed Swift's book
The Chronological History of Key West

Bodies being pulled out of the mangroves, it was reported, were swelling in the heat and sun. Finally, piles of corpses had to be covered with kerosene and torched to avoid contagion. Albert told me that some of the bodies reacting to the flames and heat were seen to crawl out of the fire.

The picture of this horror in my active child's imagination gave me nightmares for months after. I even fancied I could smell the bodies burning (maybe I did!?) when low black clouds came floating down from the North.

One of my mother's friends, an older man who was an eccentric loner, had ordered a barometer from Abercrombie and Fitch in New York. When it arrived on what became one of the last trains from the mainland, its needle was pointing to 'Hurricane' and he thought the instrument had been broken in transit! Being a recluse, he hadn't heard any of the messages of storm warning. When the hurricane struck, he climbed up and lashed himself to his tallest coconut palm and rode out the storm. They found him two days later, semi-conscious and still up the tree. He had been stripped naked by the wind, dazed but quite alive, he was still clutching the barometer.

On the fourth morning after the storm, Sophie came dancing into my grandparents' living room, her reserved calm and dignified manner completely abandoned to the wonderful news. Regis had survived! He had helped the fishing lodge owners nail down and get ready for the blow. Then, with a fifteen-foot wall of water heading toward them on the horizon, the lodge owners had turned to their staff and said, "Now every man for himself. God help us." That was the last of all of them in the rush of water. Regis was washed in a fury out to sea, swimming violently to find air and keep afloat in the churning water. Somehow he lashed himself to a huge spar with his rope belt and finally passed out. Three days later, he awoke to find himself in a hospital bed in Miami. The patrolling Coast Guard, looking for survivors had spotted and rescued him.

To Sophie, the mainland was another continent when she announced triumpantly in great pride and joy, "My grandson done swam all the way to Miami! My grandson done swam all the way to Miami!" Regis was surely a champion survivor!

Hurricane Coming

Human Hottenin'

ophie Brown, the cook, and I were sitting together under a shoreline palm tree looking up at the afternoon cocktail party in progress on the upper deck of my grandparents' houseboat, The Idler. A sea breeze was blowing in as it always does at the head of the Island, stirring the channel waters of Cow Key to deep opal and jade greens. Clouds billowed and sea birds floated and dived on the far horizon. It was a typical Florida mid-winter afternoon, balmy and beautiful. The Porter's guests, who had arrived in unexpected quantity, were all feeling lighter than air, too, from the great rum daiquiris and dry martinis that Will Porter had concocted and that were being passed by Annette, the maid, on the upper deck.

"What makes people all jam together like that?" I wondered out loud, age six or seven, to Sophie who I was sure knew all the secret wisdoms of the ages.

As we watched, the top-heavy boat tilted precariously as the

Houseboat Idler anchored at the head of the Island

crowd moved in an animated cluster to bunch together in another part of the upper deck. No one aboard seemed to notice. But watching from shore, I could easily imagine the ladies' large pastel chiffon hats floating away in the Cow Key channel, and their luminous dresses swirling and sinking down into the water . . . see it happening in slow motion: the boat going over sideways, slowly-slowly, and the ladies falling languidly and gracefully into the water, disappearing into the green depths.

The boat righted itself again and then gradually began to list toward its other side. Albert Atwell, the boatman in charge, seated under a nearby palm, rose slowly to his feet, attentive and watching.

The crowd oblivious and gay were enjoying themselves enormously. Only Scott and Zelda were missing to complete the scene of "A Last Hurrah."

"How come they crowd so close together like that, Sophie?" I asked my companion who was dozing beside me again.

Sophie opened her eyes and squinted up at the collection of revelers on the upper deck, "They jus' likes human hottenin'" she explained sleepily.

"That's what parties is for, chile."

Sun & Sand Beach Club by Wallace Kirke
A favorite gathering spot where "The Reach" is today.

Treasure

Hunt Harris' Treasure Island
J.Y. Porter's Treasure
Lucky Number
Pink Gold

Pirates! Pirates!!

Hunt Harris' Treasure Island
As Told to and Recorded by George Murphy, with my appreciation

When I was a little girl in the early '30s everybody in Key West had a treasure story. One of the best came from my fascinating neighbor, Miss Irene Johnson, who was known as the Queen of the Wreckers. She lived on Whitehead Street, just around the corner, and our back gardens (410 Caroline Street — Heritage House) shared the same property line and a side garden gate.

Miss Irene was full of wonderful stories that entranced me. She showed me a site cut into the native coral rock on our shared property line that she said was a pirate's grave. It had produced three doubloons and a rusty dagger along with human bones, a sure sign, she said, that treasure lay nearby. Miss Irene had also seen maps that indicated treasure buried in either or both of our yards. I, of course, began to dig holes all over our back garden and am still doing it.

However, an uncle of mine who lived next door on the other property side did find treasure, in an unexpected way, and this is how it all happened.

His name was Hunt Harris. Hunt's family - as was true of most families in the South - had just gone through the Civil War and come out the other side almost penniless, so they couldn't afford to send him to medical school as they had planned. It had been a major disappointment.

Hunt, however, was a resourceful individual and decided that the next best recourse was to read for the law (as it was called). To this purpose, he signed on as a lighthouse keeper, taking all of the law books required and going off for three years to study in solitude.

When he returned, he passed the bar exam and eventually became not only one of the leading lawyers on the island, but a very respected judge in the county court and President of the Florida Senate.

However, his interest in medicine never really left him and led him often to defend or assist legally in medical cases. One person whom Hunt had helped legally was an old Danish fisherman who, in gratitude when he was dying, gave Hunt a Florida Keys treasure map. He assured Hunt that it was the map to a real treasure island, and Hunt had no reason to doubt him.

In those days (circa 1900) in order to own an island in U.S. territory, all one had to do was claim it officially. Hunt took all the necessary legal precautions and did this. Once accomplished, he took into his confidence a friend who had a boat. Both men hesitated to tell their wives what they intended to do - go on a treasure hunt - knowing that their practical spouses would consider the whole matter a ridiculous and childish adventure.

So they set off on the pretense of going on a fishing trip. For a week they steamed up and down the Keys searching for the island shown on the map but found nothing. Then just as they were about to give up, as fate would have it, they ran into another Danish fisherman and showed him the map. He was immediatelyable to translate the Danish names and revealed that the small Treasure Key was quite close and within just a few miles of where they were.

Heading toward it they arrived at a lagoon on the west side of the Island, anchored and then proceeded, a la Treasure Island fashion, a number of paces inland to a higher knoll. They could feel their hearts beat faster when they sighted large coral boulders and a grove of ancient sea grape trees indicated on the spot marked X on the map. They began to dig down and down until their shovels hit the top of a large object that became an old sea chest. Frantically they uncovered it and broke open the rusted, jammed lid to look inside. Empty !

As small compensation, under the chest they found one forgotten, rusted silver coin, but real enough to show their wives and fend off the teasing they knew they would recieve when they returned home.

A few years passed and Henry Flagler was headed towards Key West with his Florida East Coast Railroad. Hunt received a letter from Flagler's chief engineer, Mr. Trumbo. After formal introduction it said: "Your island is conveniently located near our projected plans for the seven mile bridge. We would like to buy sand from you collected from the tidal inlet on your island. Please let us hear from you as soon as possible."

Hunt responded immediately saying, "Mr. Flagler is welcome to all the sand he can use. Please help yourself."

Trumbo responded with thanks but added, "Mr. Flagler doesn't do business that way," and sent him a check for $1,000.

It so happened that the island was situated at the edge of a deep water channel and as fast as the sand was dredged out, it came back in. Flagler kept using it and regular checks were sent in payment. Hunt had found at least some treasure in his Island. With the event of the railroad opening up possibilities, the Keys began to flourish and develop. An entrepreneur approached Hunt with the idea of opening a fishing lodge and marine harbour and bought the island by paying a deposit of fifty percent of the price, with the balance to be paid over a time. However, shortly after the buyer suddenly died. His estate was settled and as he had paid only half the purchase price, the island was returned to Harris.

Time passed and along came the Great Depression. The government, to create jobs, had decided to open and enlarge the inland waterway. They approached Hunt for the riparian rights for the needed project and Hunt sold the Island again.

So, in a sense, it really was Hunt's "Treasure Island" and in the end, this money went to establish a grandson's education, his family couldn't afford for Harris so many years earlier.

The Overseas Highway to Key West

J. Y. Porter's Treasure

When I was a child growing up here in Key West in the '30s, all one had to do was mention "treasure" and everyone had a story to tell in return.

My favorite older cousin, J.Y. Porter, IV, successful lawyer and very popular personage here on the island, responded like this: "If anyone discovers a cache of gold coins and gold bars worth now over a million dollars, just know it belongs to me!"

Having staked his claim, he would tell this story: His grandfather (Dr. Porter), along with everyone else in town, before we had banks on the Island, always hid their money somewhere in the house. In Dr. Porter's case, it was kept in a trundle bed secreted beneath his big double bed in a safe box.

"One evening, Grandfather Porter and Grandmother Louisa returned from a party to see a disappearing figure rushing out the gate of their side garden on Duval. They recognized him as an employee of their relative, wrecker Stephen Lowe. The runaway was a man named John Ward, and he was seen carrying a metal box under his arm as he retreated.

Suspecting the worst, they rushed into their house and up the stairs to find that, indeed, their money box had been stolen from its hiding place, and without a doubt, the fleeing figure had taken it. Knowing the thief could only make his getaway by sea, Dr. Porter hurried to his neighbors for help. They knew that Ward would most probably take a fishing vessel belonging to his

J. Y. Porter IV

employer to use for escape. Down to the waterfront they rushed with a crowd of supporters and arrived just in time to see the sails set and the boat heading out into the Gulf. In hot pursuit, they finally caught up, boarded the ship and captured the culprit. But where was the stolen money? Not aboard the ship anywhere. When and where had the thief had time to stash it, or had he, seeing capture inevitable, thrown it over the side of the ship into the shallows?

The trial was held within a few days and the thief was condemned to prison. No one, however, could ever make him disclose what he had done with the stolen money. He was sentenced to ten years at the state prison at Tallahassee.

They said Ward endured his term stoically, even though the jail food lacked everything except just enough nourishment to keep a man alive.All during that time he yearned for and dreamed of his favorite dish — chicken..

Fellow prisoners said later, that he boasted continuously about how he would be a rich man when he was finally released. Ten years passed. Having paid his debt to society with his term completed, he could not be punished again, and the stolen wealth would be his without any further penalty.

On the afternoon of his release, Ward headed first for a plantation farm in the near vicinity. That night, he broke into its chicken yard, was discovered by the owner, and was shot dead on the spot.

Telling this story, J.Y. would draw in his breath and look threateningly around at his audience with a glint of fierceness and suppressed humor, "So if anyone finds my grandfather's cache of gold bars and coins valued at more than $ 1,000,000 by now, just remember . . . It's mine!!"

*   *   *

J.Y. looked radiant, "after ten years with no break, I'm finally taking a vacation," he informed me, overflowing with more than his usual exuberance. I was immediately curious. Where would this hard working bon vivant go? New York? Rio? Perhaps Paris? "Where are you headed J.Y?" I asked. "Mud Key!" he responded joyfully, almost shouting with delight.

Lucky Number

Key West has always been an island of many voices. Animal, vegetable and mineral. Sounds have a strange way here. They can originate in one spot and be picked up and teleported by breeze to another, sometimes over a mile apart.

In the old days, cocks crowing, both night and day, but especially in the dead of night, came from feisty, fighting game cocks that were as long-legged as ostriches and as beplumed and multicolored as exotic game birds. While the roosters and the cats made the orchestral night music, the most persistent chorus by day came from the Cuban orphans' voices carried over radio waves from Havana calling out the winning lottery numbers.

It was a code, a melodious, rhythmic chant — Deee Deee De De De Deee Deee Deee, a singsong of winning numbers that during the Depression, could spell out a fortune in thousands of pesos or dollars, or so it was hoped, believed and occasionally realized. Everybody played the lottery!

Che Che, the popular owner of Che Che's bar on Division

Street (now Truman Avenue) was sitting on his sidewalk bench in front of his establishment one hot morning waiting for the Greyhound bus to come by and drop off a packet from Miami, when an old man wandered listlessly into its path, and was struck and killed instantly.

The message of what numbers to bet on in that day's bolita was shockingly delivered, but clear! Old man (90), bus (46), and Big Death (88). He invested and won $10,000, I believe, a fortune in 1933 Key West!

A few more numbers from the lottery tables include 38 = money, 21 = pregnant, 30 = man, 3 = sailor, 12 = woman, 12 = prostitute, 47 = birds, 49 = gays, 13 = gigolo, 16 = horned (cuckold), 15 = dog, 13 = scorpion, 4 − cat, 11 = rooster, 14 = cemetery, 88 = Big Death, 2 = butterfly, 49 = drunk, 27 = bee, 20 = cup (or toilet seat).

These lottery numbers were given to me by 'Benito' (Antonio) Ramoes, while at our favorite unisex hair salon on White Street. Juanita's Beauty Salon is a small enclave of surviving Conch culture still intact.

Recently and tragically Benito was struck and killed instantly by a motor bike on North Roosevelt Boulevard. But I know he is playing bolita in heaven now and winning his heart's desire.

Juanita

Pink Gold

The dramatic discovery in Key West waters of 'Pink Gold', as shrimps were called, had all the excitement and intrigue of a Klondike Gold Rush. The story as I know it, started in the mid-'40s with a young ichthyologist on vacation swimming in the waters of the Sun & Sand, a popular beach club that was located where The Reach is now.

Idly he picked up a clump of floating sargasso seaweed, throwing it out of his way, and watched with interest and then amazement as hundreds of tiny shrimp, hiding in its density, were suddenly revealed in the water. From their minuscule size he realized at once that they were only a few hours old, and that they must be hatching in beds off Key West and very nearby.

He had a few days vacation and time to explore this fascinating possibility, so he took himself over to Thompson Enterprises. Thompson was the largest commercial fishery on the island. There he found owners Norberg, Karl, Charles and Jack. Telling them his theory, he convinced them to use one of their fishing boats to go search for the beds where he believed the shrimp must be hatching.

Up to this time, shrimp had been caught in this area only in limited quantities, just enough for the local market.

I remember being driven along the boulevard on hot summer evenings with my family, "catching the breeze" and seeing the waters off East Martello Tower dotted with small dinghies and sail boats. It

Turtle crawls - Key West - Thompson Enterprise

was a pretty sight. Kerosene or battery lamps were mounted on their sterns and they cast gleaming cone-shaped lights down into the water to attract the shrimp. Hand nets were used to scoop them up and into the boat.

Years ago, on the East Coast, fried shrimp were not that popular, as I remember. They were considered, along with mullet, mostly just good bait. But the sea-dependent Conchs made great enchiladas from them. Sophie, my grandparent's fine cook, created wonderful dishes with shrimp, usually served over rice. But it wasn't until the 40s that shrimp emerged as a delicacy on sophisticated tables and in gourmet restaurants in New York and San Francisco. Perhaps what really helped to launch this delicious crustacean commercially inland was the advent of frozen foods, first started by Birdseye. And it stabilized the market, even in an off season, for the shrimpers who were forced to grin and bear a pre-set market price, or get out of the business. Later, many did.

To return to our hero, the young ichthyologist who had convinced Thompson Enterprises to go out shrimp fishing: They

Sailors enjoying the shrimp boats

trolled the waters off Key West for several days, throwing out nets and pulling them in, always empty except for hundreds of small fish, which are still the unfortunate casualties of this industry. But no luck — no shrimp at all.

Meantime, a Humphrey Bogart type, a loner, a shark fisherman (shark liver was used medicinally and sold commercially for iron deficiency) living up on the Keys, got wind that something was up. He enjoyed eavesdropping on his short wave radio for entertainment, listening to the fishing boats talk back and forth to each other during the day, and communicating with their shore bases on this band. By the fourth day, after dragging the bottom with no success, the Thompson crew was ready to give up and go home. It was well into evening, after a long day of disappointment, and quite dark when they started to turn back to Key West.

The ichthyologist asked to throw the baby net out for one last try — just for luck. When they started to pull it back in, it almost broke with the heaviness of its catch! It was loaded with shrimp! The secret of shrimping was discovered! Shrimp bury themselves deep

Shrimp boats - Key West

in the sand during the day, and come to the surface of the sea bottom to feed at night. Only then can they be netted and caught.

Meantime, the excitement in their voices over the radio, announcing to home base, "We got um, we've struck it rich," was picked up by the eavesdropping shark fisherman. Thompson tried to keep the news secret, but "Bogart" up on the Keys had caught the scent of a bonanza and further eavesdropping convinced him that the "Mother Lode" had been discovered. He high-tailed it up to a competitive fishing business in Tampa and alerted them to the discovery. Even before Thompson's boats were fully galvanized to begin to shrimp commercially, competitive operators had arrived on the scene and begun shrimping the night waters off Key West.

Word spread like wildfire on the wind from coast to coast, and the town suddenly looked like and found itself in the midst of a bonanza gold rush — Pink Gold! Fishermen and boats came from everywhere, from both sides of the continent; from Nova Scotia to Oregon, en masse. The hunt was on! And Key West found itself back in the fishing business again — big time!

*   *   *

EPILOGUE

Shrimping never had a "season" or any restrictions. The industry maintained that shrimp not only bred in sandy-bottomed areas, but in areas with coral and rock formation, where it was impossible to fish for them because of resultant net damage. The rationale was that they were protected naturally. This attitude was only partially true, and did not prevent over-shrimping in our area. But we Key Westers should try shimping, again off Martello on South Roosevelt Blvd. Brush off your battery lanterns and dinghy. And let's go!

Thompson's Turtle Kraals

Cuban Key West

Snuggler's Cove
Spanish Music
Fighting Cocks
Lucignani

A Key West Collection by Marthe Watson Sauer

Snuggler' Cove

For years, a big sign rested on the ground against the kapok tree on the front lawn of our county courthouse on Whitehead Street, declaring triumphantly:

END OF THE RAINBOW

End of U.S. HWY 1

CITY JAIL

I am sure the city organization that produced this sign complimented itself on never missing an opportunity to promote up and coming Key West.

Down on Front Street another such inspired advertisement were two signs hanging side by side on the windows of two companion shops, "Wedding Licenses Furnished Here" and next to it another declaring "Mattresses for Sale".

In the 30s and 40s, because of very, very low city budgets, jail inmates were not only allowed but encouraged to go home to their families for dinner. If they didn't return by eleven o'clock in the evening, they got locked out of the jail for the night!

West Martello Tower, now the Joe Allen Garden Center, which

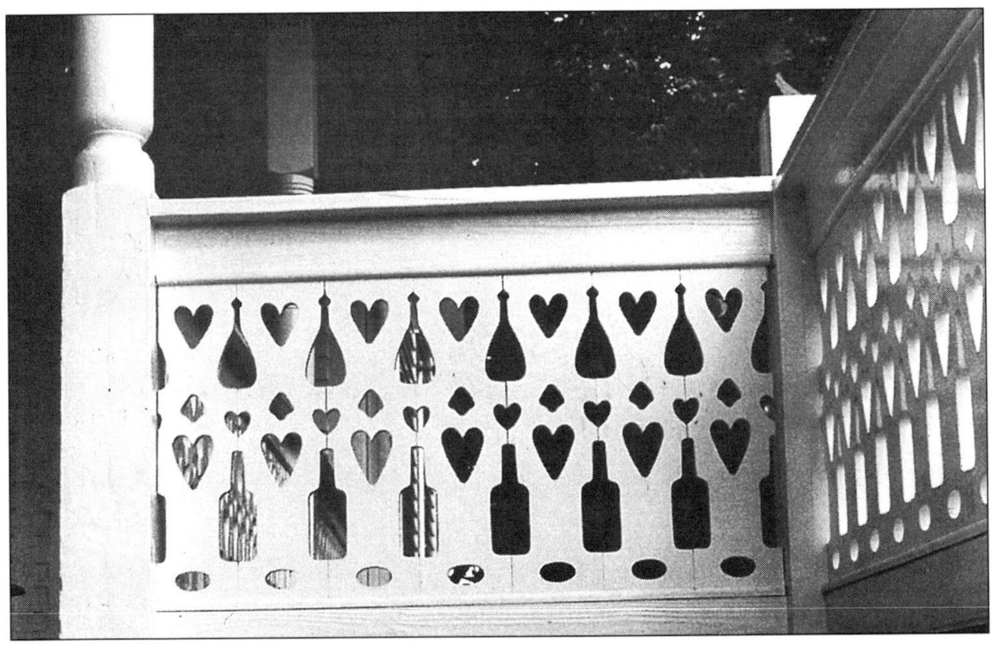

Speakeasy balustrade - cognac and whiskey, hearts and diamonds

was our earliest Art and Historical Society meeting place, was restored by temporarily jailed plumbers, brick-layers and electricians while they were doing time. Often, work had to be held up for weeks because a needed mason or electrician wasn't incarcerated, and work would have to wait until they were thrown in the drink again.

Raul Vasquez and his brother, members of a delightful Key West Cuban family, were proprietors of a very popular speakeasy on Duval Street during Prohibition days (now called Speakeasy Inn). One can identify the house today with its front-porch gingerbread design showing openings in the balustrade shaped like whiskey and cognac bottles and smaller hearts and diamonds.

For the most part, the island population, known as "Conchs," utterly ignored Prohibition. Key West was just too near Cuba and too far removed from that "foolishness up on the Mainland."

Delicious Bacardi and Anejo rum was too cheap, and Key West was too much of a social drinking town.

So the system that was established was efficient and simple: when a "Government Man" would step aboard the Overseas Railroad in Miami to come down to inspect, an observer, always on duty at the station, would immediately telegraph ahead to Key West to close all the "shops." The train took several hours to arrive, plenty of time for liquor to be secreted away in wells and between floors or walls or in backyard outhouses. Plenty of time to convert the tables and shelves to display bottles of Old Sour, homemade root beer and ginger-ale or condensed milk along with condiments and Shakespeare, and transform the place into domino and card parlors.

However, the Vasquez brothers, who were very gregarious, gracious and social, were not always on guard. One afternoon in the late 20s, an affable "Government Man" in plain clothes got through the net, stepped off the train unnoticed and went into their speakeasy. He was received warmly, took a long thirsty drink of rum and promptly arrested both brothers. A trial was set and held with the courtroom overflowing with family and sympathetic friends. The Judge, who had been one of their best customers, very apologetically sentenced them to the lightest term possible. He gave them, I believe, one month, and with much embracing and handshaking all around, told them that they could move into the jail at their convenience. They were to include their families and needed furniture and to make themselves as comfortable as possible. This they did the next day, fourteen in all, which included only the youngest children and some domestic help. The whole episode was treated as a holiday, a family outing, and they celebrated it each afternoon with a cocktail party to which they invited their many Key West friends, including the Judge.

An old friend who once owned a bar/speakeasy in Prohibition days recounts that rumrunners actually created a system of rationing so all the bars in town would get a fair and equal share of what was smuggled in from Cuba and elsewhere.

Monroe County Courthouse - Key West by Wallace Kirke

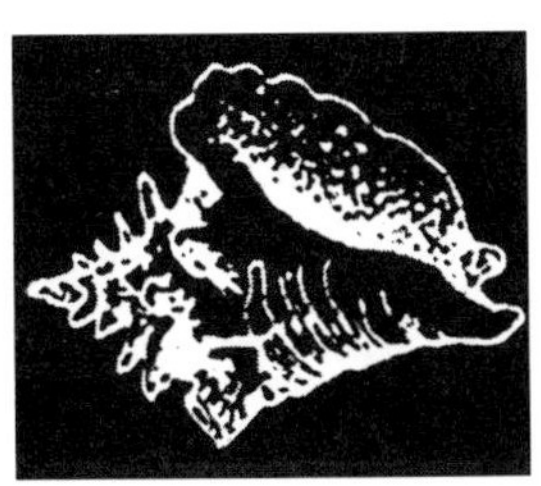

Spanish Music

ariano came from Basque country in Spain. He had been hired there by the richest man in his small village in the mountains to teach his daughters how to play the guitar — an instrument Mariano played to perfection. He also had perfect pitch and could tune anything that made music. The rich landowner didn't know or had forgotten the tale of Orpheus, because he was surprised and furious when the youngest of his three sheltered girls, Inez, fell in love with the dreamy musician. She persuaded the guitarist to run away with her to see the New World. Elopement, she knew, was the only way that they could ever escape the village. Her father would never allow her to marry down to Mariano's status as just the village musician.

So they eloped in the depths of the Esturian night, with Inez's three brothers following in hot pursuit by cock's crow the next morning. Inez was unexpectedly resourceful and wily in eluding them, and at length the two arrived at the ramparts of the ocean, so vast, so limitless to Mariano that he stood wide-eyed gazing in awe. The enormity and expanse of it was such a contrast from their mountain bound village! He felt overwhelmed.

What to do next? But again Inez solved the problem, for in the folds of her petticoats she had secreted gold coins and with some of these they were able to buy passage to Cuba and safety. In Cuba, both worked very hard, and from their savings they bought their passage to Key West. Here Inez took in laundry while Mariano played the guitar at Pena's Garden of Roses and at Raul's (where Martha's is on the Boulevard today), and tuned pianos on the Island.

Eventually, they had several children and settled into a comfortable house. Life became generous and good except for one thing — Inez had taken a lover, and a very indiscreet one at that. The pair not only met each other publicly when ever they chose, but the lover, a cigar factory owner, would often drive by in his sport car, park it at the curb in front of their house, sound the horn and wait impatiently for Inez to join him in it. Mariano's peaceful, dreamy nature was pushed to the limits of its endurance.

One evening, the lover drove up, parked in front of the house as usual, and sounded his horn. This time, the vibration of that sound — tinny, grating — went straight into Mariano's brain like a hot drill. With a cry of rage and anguish he rushed to the bathroom, grabbed his straight-edged razor and arrived on the curb in a flash. The lover barely had time to extract himself from Inez's embrace when the razor made its way downward from under his chin to his belt buckle and he was laid wide open to the last daylight he or his body would ever remember.

When the jury tried the case the verdict was quick and certain: NOT GUILTY. Who wouldn't have killed one's wife's lover in the act of betrayal at one's own curb?!!

Inez, who had worn the pants for all too long all those years, felt her love for Mariano revive and burst into torrents of passion.

A man who would kill for you must love you beyond reason! It was all she needed to settle down and live contentedly with him for the rest of their lives.

Guitarist by Susie dePoo

Fighting Cocks – Susie dePoo – 1997

Fighting Cocks

One of my favorite childhood playmates who lived around the corner, in other words, "the boy next door," was Johnny DeP. He was the mischievous imp of the Island whom everybody knew and enjoyed with a "What's next?" attitude. Our forbidden games included climbing the Navy yard radio towers: where my hands froze into the metal at 200 feet while Johnny blissfully mounted to the top totally unafraid; we had afternoons of catching crawfish in the swirling tides and down-currents under the Porter docks; and happily smoking Wing cigarettes (a nickel a pack) in my big tree-house in the gumbo-limbo and sea grape trees, i.e. generally misbehaving with a totally concentrated joy during a lot of our childhood.

Johnny's step-father was the much admired Dr. DeP who, apart from being a fine physician, was one of the handsomest men on the island. If one would compare him to movie actors of his day, the nearest resemblance and type would be Cesar Romero, a suave charmer. Dr. DeP had large dark brown eyes glowing with warmth and sympathy, a straight handsome nose, and a black

mustache that began and ended where it should. His high broad forehead was crested with thick glossy black hair that fell over it in a bang like a beckoning finger. He stood well over six feet tall with an athletic, broad-shouldered, slim-waisted elegance that came alive with music. He was a wonderful dancer. When he and his attractive and diminutive blond first wife, Bel, dined and danced together al fresco in the gardens of the Casa Marina on Saturday evenings, everyone stood back to watch them and enjoy. The two were better than Ginger Rogers and Fred Astaire . . . at least we all thought so.

However, with all these additions and attractions to his credit, apart from his medical practice, which he took very seriously giving it his utmost dedication and devotion, his great passion and hobby on the side was cock fighting. Perhaps it was the beauty of the cocks that had attracted him originally to this bloody and violent sport; perhaps the intense do-or-die energy of the cocks themselves; or the utterly steeled concentration of nerves and energy of the victor, with head and neck arched, bending triumphantly over a bowed and humiliated opponent. Something primordial and distinctly cruel ran parallel with the healing instincts of the good doctor.

Dr. DeP's cocks were known to be among the finest game fighters on the island. Their gamekeeper, Gregario, was the best, training the cocks by rolling barrels under them to teach balance, and feeding them only corn and wheat kernals of special quality. Gregario's task was also keeping the male birds away from the hen yards, allowing them entrance only on specified occasions, but never just before their scheduled fights. This privation kept their warring competitive spirits at a hot and urgent boiling point.

It was no surprise and of much interest to cock fight aficionados on the island that the doctor had ordered two more birds from Trinidad, reported to be of the highest caliber of championship quality. These expensive cocks, whose lincage, it was claimed, went back to the Conquistadors in Spain, would undoubtedly be sure winners.

The cock fight arena in Key West in those days was well known, but well hidden. It was located on the small side street across from the Cuban Club that faces Duval, and surrounded by high board fences that flanked the narrow yards of several small Cuban cigar workers' houses. These cottages, whose "shotgun" hallways ran from front door to back, looked directly into several heavily populated, well-scratched and dark-earthed chicken yards, full of the clucking sounds of their female occupants and the constant bugling and crowing of their flamboyant mates.

Entering this world from the street was like entering the world of the Minotaur, through passageways of high boarded labyrinthine fences leading to a miniature amphitheater at the center. Tiers of rustic plank seats formed an intimate circle beneath a corrugated tin roof. From its high open sides beneath the roof, brilliant shafts of dusty gold sunlight flooded down on the arena floor. Cocks illuminated in these shafts were breath-takingly beautiful. Some were mullet-colored and plumed with swirling cascading tails that were jet black or white, some with cream-colored spotted wings, some snow-flaked and others wine colored; breasts that had flourishes of iridescent jade, and ruby capes around necks of peaked and pointed feathers. All this glory was crowned with cock-combs and wattles of tomato red and tangerine orange, pulsating with fighting blood. Their angry snake-like glances flicked this way and that, fastening on an adversary with intense unswerving hatred.

At the entrance of the arena, there generally stood a large and rotund policeman in full uniform, supposedly posted there to keep, if not the law, then order, since fights could and did break out between the owners of the winners and losers.

The Saturday of Dr. DeP's much anticipated roosters' entrée into the Key West cock fight world arrived. The doctor's reputation had never soared higher in the sporting world of Key West, and wagers were never more intense or odds higher than those in favor of Dr. DeP's much-publicized Trinidad cocks. All promises and prospects probably would have been fulfilled with far greater rewards (mostly prestigious for the doctor), had his stepson, my friend Johnny, not taken it into his impish head to participate in this "Commedia del Arte."

Very early that morning, Johnny had let the two pecan-fed but love-starved cocks into the hen yards, where they had had their way with every hen in the area. By that afternoon, when they were unleashed with much fanfare into the fighting ring, they staggered in like two exhausted and satiated boulevardiers wobbling down The Paseo de Madrid, much preferring to love than to fight.

Needless to say, Doctor De P's reputation as a cock fighting impresario never recouped after this fiasco, and it will always remain a black day in the annals of Key West cock fighting.

Lucignani

Lucignani's was a favorite watering spot and ice cream parlor on the island, up by the Cuban Club on Duval, especially on hot summer nights. His tropical ices and ice creams were famous all around the Caribbean and the Keys: tamarind, sapodilla, soursop (guyabana), guava, coconut, and Key Lime were fresh from local trees that grew on the Island — they all tasted like ambrosia.

Lucignani was a creative but sensible man. When his Key Lime ice was discovered as a wonderful base for frozen daiquiris, first probably by Hemingway's crowd, and then by the FERA artists and visitors on the Island, the run on it was so fierce and aggressive that he was heard to say resignedly, "If this here Key Lime ice gets any more popular, I'm just going to have to discontinue it!"

Such was life and wisdom in Key West in the 30s and early 40s.

*   *   *

Dan and Ellie McConnell of Flamingo Crossing, across Duval Street from where Lucignani's once was, are keeping up the tradition of tropical ices and ice creams in grand style today.

If one compares the taste of tropical fruited ices and ice creams to music, one can say they are in a minor key to our tastebuds rather than in the major like apples, and pears, etc. and more subtle in flavor.

The site of Lucignani's ice cream parlor

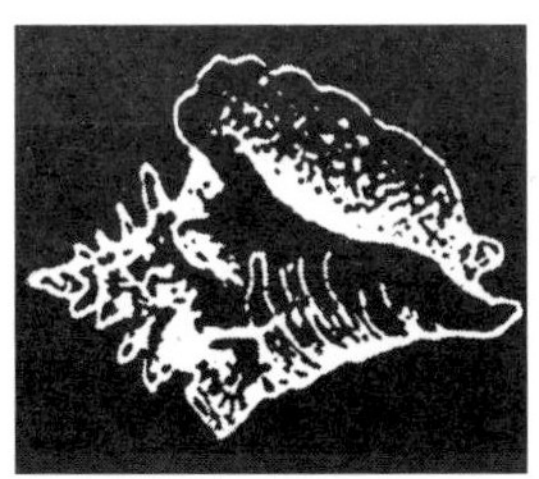

More Stories

Committee of 100
Bad Dog
Sunday Service
The Heron and the Turtle
Indians and Wayfarers

Florida Motorist Magazine
left to right: Governor Dave Sholtz, F.D.R. and Jules Stone

The Committee of One Hundred

lizabeth Cooper was a plain-looking hard-working, feisty little dynamo, such a contrast to her handsome and distinguished husband. Yet it was she who was the force and energy, the enmeshing glue, that held together the Committee of One Hundred; the illustrious millionaire group that met each winter in Miami during the 1920s and 30s. It seemed millionaires very much enjoyed being in each other's company. There was no question or danger of being pursued or liked for one's money alone. They all had plenty of the green stuff.

Clayton Cooper made a wonderful figurehead for this group with his wavy white hair, baby pink complexion and calm, blue-eyed regality. He was the benevolent deuce who ruled over their play and games in hard earned Paradise. And Miami in the late 20s and 30s was surely a millionaire's paradise! Boating parties, tango and rumba lessons, wild pig stalking in the Everglades and group trips to the Bahamas where one could throw money at roulette wheels. Win or lose, it didn't much matter. Most of the brethren were workaholics who had never had time to learn to play or to have fun and were now weathering out the depression, and Clayton was certainly the man who knew how, with unquestionable style and panache.

Their wives were equally pleased with well-organized social get togethers: Rabalaian costume balls and dances at the Roney Plaza and the Biltmore; bridge parties and open limousine rides in the afternoons along the water roads of the beach were what they had always dreamt of, but most hadn't known how to acquire. Behind all this rich man's pleasure world, few of the members bothered to realize that it was the energetic, homely Elizabeth who arranged and orchestrated everything.

One evening during a fancy dress ball at the Biltmore, Harry Osborne, dressed as Henry VIII, dropped over on a high kick in the midst of a Conga line and was carried off the floor to a small side vestibule where minutes later he died of a coronary. It was so sudden and clean that most of the other members envied him, hoping that their own ends would be as quick and easy. His wife Lucille, however, felt otherwise. It was well known by most of the other members that Harry had been a womanizer, with several mistresses, and that he had also had a proclivity for show girls on the side. These occasional past indiscretions had always been covered and disposed of by Elizabeth. Whether Lucille actually knew of Harry's weakness or not was questionable but probable. Nonetheless, her grief knew no bounds and was set off at any provocation and at every turn. "Poor dear Harry," she would wail, "Loved oysters so!" at seeing them listed as an appetizer on a menu, or, "Darling Harry, what will I do without him! He organized everything" during a bridge game. At the height of this particular balmy winter season, she had draped herself in widow's weeds, black from head to Saks Fifth Avenue pumps, and her perspiring brow and face were often clouded and tear shining behind veils of Spanish lace. This period of mourning continued unremittingly for weeks until Elizabeth, her prime caretaker, was pushed to the limits of endurance.

She finally had to make a break for it and came down to Key West to her friends Grace and Jessie. As was her custom, she arrived on the Overseas Railroad, bringing with her one small valise of clothes — she could always borrow, if need be, from her hostesses — and a much larger suitcase stuffed with good books to read and to share for their pleasure. When they greeted her at the station she looked exhausted. "There is nothing," she declared with conviction as she stepped off the train, "truly as dear as a newly dead husband!"

(Far Left) Will Porter, Key West Mayor Willy DeMeritt, and Miss Jessie (far right) meet visiting dignitaries at the Overseas Railroad station in Key West

Bad Dog

The South has always had a tradition of oral history and storytelling. It was meant to entertain and enchant, but especially to teach wisdoms and lessons in life. The Uncle Remus tales by Joel Chandler Harris do that superbly, but need to be "translated" for today's readers. Their Victorian Negro dialect is almost as difficult as Shakespearean English is to the modern ear. One of the Uncle Remus stories, the one about the ne'er-do-well and the hungry puppy, is a classic. It goes like this:

A tramp or drifter is headed for his favorite bar when he almost stumbles over an abandoned puppy in the gutter. The puppy licks his boot straps and follows him into the bar where the drifter throws him a tidbit of jerky offered free to the bar's customers. When he leaves, the dog follows him home to a make-shift shanty where they take up residence together.

Each day the grateful puppy follows him to the bar and is given scraps thrown to him by his adopted master. This goes on for some time until the man, because of his derelict life, falls ill.

Desperate for food for both of them the dog manages to steal from various town sources, and is finally caught by the authorities.

The lesson the story teaches is that the dog was noble and good in every way: he was loyal, faithful, loving, grateful, inventive, and courageous. But he had one fatal flaw and failure, he had chosen a poor master and it had made a thief of him.

Center: Wallace & Jessie Kirke - 1930

Sunday Service

The minister of the church, after many years of tenure, had died in harness and the church Deacons appointed themselves to scout for a replacement. "Let's take our time. Let's not be in a hurry," they cautioned each other, knowing full well from past experience how lifetime long a commitment could become.

They contacted a ministerial bureau for potential and available clergymen with the idea of hearing a number of them speak before making any final selection.

Each Sunday one of the Deacons would meet the train of the incoming contender and take him by buggy to church. The whole congregation would listen attentively, chat and feel him out after the service, and return him to the departing train. Several months passed in this fashion without any really strong contenders or positive reactions from the congregation. In the third month there came a potential churchman that the whole congregation responded to positively. Although he seemed just right, they warned the interviewing Deacon to speak to him about his expectations without making a definite commitment, and invite him to return. In the buggy ride back to the train station the Deacon began.

"Reverend, we really enjoyed your sermon this morning and we would like you to come back again. Would you be willing to do this on a trial basis? Say, for several Sundays? After all, you will want to know more about us and the town and the general circumstances; see how we all get along together. Would you be willing to do this for several Sundays, while we all consider, and how much would you charge?"

The visiting Reverend thought a moment and then responded. "Well, I have a tremendous sermon, moving and spiritually very powerful for fifty dollars. I have another sermon that is simple but profound and moving for forty dollars. I have another message that is very basic and down to earth but inspiring for thirty dollars and I have still another that gets to the basics, points out needed lessons for fifteen dollars. I have another for five dollars, but frankly Deacon, it's not worth a Damn."

Remembering this story, when the family emerged from a church service together, they would often comment to each other, "That was certainly a fifty dollar sermon — really good!" or, "I'd say that was about a twenty, wouldn't you?" or, "Frankly, that wasn't worth a damn."

The Heron and the Turtle

 haughty blue heron preening himself while standing in the shallow waters of the Everglades, turned to a mud turtle sunning himself nearby on the bank of a hammock.

"Why is it," he asked of the turtle looking down on him disdainfully, "that in an hour I can fly further than you can crawl in an entire lifetime?" The turtle, undaunted, blinked his eyes in the bright Florida sunshine and swallowed his chagrin.

"Because," he replied calmly, "I take such pleasure in going so slowly."

(With thanks to La Fontaine.)

Indians and Wayfarers

The first actors in the sea drama to leave their mark on the Island's mystique were the Calusa and Tequesta, and later the Seminole Indians. They were known to paddle in their dugout canoes fifty miles a day from the mainland down through the Keys stopping at trading spots along the way. Key West was the last watering spot and largest post before the longer paddle to Cuba.

It is interesting to note that Heritage House is located on a large mound, an Indian kitchen midden of shells left by the Indians who camped here. The property has an outpouring of fresh spring water that comes from an underground stream that traverses the island and was later converted into a well by seafarers and pirates. The well is still operative today in Heritage House's front yard.

When the Spanish first arrived, they reported that they found large quantities of human bones, both on the ground and in trees.

Ponce de Leon "Glimpsing Paradise"

Victorious Indians would hardly have placed their enemies' remains in trees, as the Spanish found them. This custom would indicate that the island was not just a battle field, but a sacred burial ground as well.

Rupert Rio, our much loved and well respected groundskeeper for many many years, told of his work at the beginning of World War II, helping to create trenches for pipe lines for the New Sound School then being constructed in the enlarged Navy yard at the end of Southard Street. He reported that they uncovered a number of bones that must have belonged to humans that were at least eight feet tall. Their leg bones were enormous, he said. I teased him that he had probably dug into an Army mule burying ground, but he insisted that he knew human remains when he saw them. It is known that Tequesta Indians were very tall — but eight feet? Is it possible? The answer may still be there under the asphalt of what is now Truman Annex.

One early spring in the 50s I was invited to go with the Audubon Society group to Fort Jefferson in the Dry Tortugas. It was the nesting season of the Sooty Terns on nearby Bush Key. My father, Wallace Kirke, then president of the society, had leased a shrimp boat to take several dozen members down there for the weekend. I accepted the invitation with relish. The trip turned out to be a memorable one for me, and I think for everyone else who went on this adventure.

First of all, Tortugas is a very interesting place to visit, just for its atmosphere alone. It is not a brooding, ominous place, as one would think, having been America's "Devil's Island" in the past. Rather, it has a "far far away" mood that makes it feel somehow off in space, rather than part of this planet. Set in magnificent opalescent water, the fort's massive warm rust-colored brick walls (now being cracked and broken by neglect and by jets breaking the sound barrier overhead), and windowed gunsights rise almost castle-like out of its surrounding moat and Gulf waters.

The group was mostly my parents' age, people whom I knew well but who were considerably older, so that on arrival I was singled out immediately by the young assistant park ranger to be shown around the premises. He was a lonely, attractive, dark-haired and high cheek-boned young man named Richard Carné (or near), and was half French, half American Indian. He was working, he told me, in his present removed circumstance, in order to save money to create an Indian museum somewhere along the east coast of Florida. As he began describing his future plans, he became more and more enthused and excited, and then confided in me that he already had the centerpiece of his collection that would make him and his museum famous worldwide.

"Let me show you some photos," he urged me. "They are in my quarters."

His "quarters" turned out to be part of the chief ranger and wife's house. My curiosity had been thoroughly aroused, even though I had no idea what he would show me. From a scarred wooden box he drew out a half-dozen well-fingered black and white photographs. In succession, the first shot revealed the outline of a long wooden ship, almost submerged in tidal mud and barely discernible. The next two photos showed the same ship, gradually being raised and revealed, about sixty feet long, with well-defined planks and ribs. Its sides had been eaten by sea worms. The last three photos zeroed in on the carved wooden figurehead at its prow. It was that of a woman with wide eyes staring in an expression of mixed fear and fierceness. Around her head and down over her forehead curled a startling collection of entwined and wreathing serpents: A Medusa stared out of the mud and at us from almost two thousand years of time!

Carné told me that he had first been contacted by a local farmer who had heard that he collected artifacts. The man's property included land on a tidal water estuary on the central east coast of Florida.

"There is a large old wooden boat, he told me, sunk deep in the mud that the last hurricane uncovered, but it had since sunk back down again. You are welcome to come see it and dig it out if you are interested," he told Richard.

"Since then," Carné told me, "I've researched its origins: I believe it's a Roman Galleon from the time of Nero — the first century A.D., when he was persecuting the Christians. Some of them must have escaped in this ship, and out of the Straits of Gibraltar. There they became caught up in the Gulf Stream, and ended up here in the tidal waters of Florida."

He continued, "I took these photographs, then sank the ship back down in the mud. It was already starting to disintegrate even in the few hours that I had it exposed — but it's safe at the moment."

"What will you do next?" I asked with genuine fascination.

Richard held the dog-eared photos and looked worried.

"Why don't you contact the Smithsonian?" I suggested.

"Never! Can't do that!" he responded emotionally. "They'll claim it, take it over and out of my hands. Besides, they probably wouldn't believe me."

"Couldn't you send them photos and a piece of wood to prove its reality and make a deal beforehand?"

"They'd analyze the mud, and know immediately exactly where the ship is located," he said with surety. "I'd lose it. I don't stand a chance, having no academic credentials, against the big boys taking over."

"Then what will you do?" I asked with concern and interest.

"I don't know yet, but I'll think of something to keep it my discovery," he said.

It seems he has succeeded in protecting his claim.

Has anyone seen or heard about a Roman Galleon found in tidewater Florida?

Roman Galleon

Welcomers

The three tall radio towers in the Navy yard were not the "bitter witnesses" that Elizabeth Bishop mentions in her poem "Late Air," but wonderful welcomers. I remember feeling my heart leap at the first sight of them from, I think, Big Pine Key, as we drove down the Keys, their amber lights blinking in the twilight afterglow as we headed back home from a summer trip.

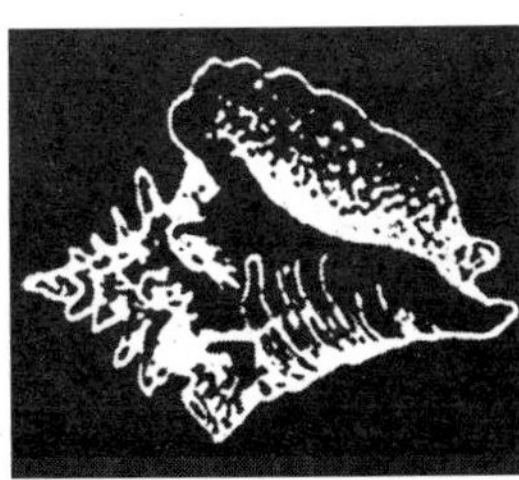

Nature

Terncoat
Key West Critters
Oil on the Water
The World is Our Garden
Key West Saturday Night

Terns

Terncoat

arl Sagan has been quoted as saying, "We are the only species that can reflect on the results and repercussions of our actions." Somehow I feel that he is underestimating most of the other species and judging their natures by our own human standards rather than by their own. This story may support that theory.

In the Dry Tortugas next to Garden Key, where Ft. Jefferson stands (and is alarmingly deteriorating today in the vibrations of jetstreams from military planes that could and should be rerouted away from it) is a small, rocky spit of coral rock and sand called Bush Key. Hardly big enough to even have a name, it is all sand and coral rock, half-submerged and half thrown up and exposed to blazing sun and Caribbean seas and wind. This almost barren little speck of creation has its cosmic connections as the sole nesting place of the sooty tern in the Northern hemisphere. It lies just across a narrow, deep, azure channel, a stone's throw from the fort. It is a mystery how sea birds, like the terns, have chosen this unlikely spot to perpetuate themselves in the universe.

Nesting terns on Bush Key

About 80,000 adult birds breed each year on Bush Key in February and early March. One egg per pair is laid in a shallow scrape on open sand or under scattered shrubs. After August, sooty terns leave the Tortugas and become strictly pelagic (sea-going) again.

Years ago a group of ornithologists from Woods Hole Laboratory came to study the terns and their nesting place to fathom their processes and secrets. They told us a very moving and alarmingly dramatic tale indeed.

The sand, even in spring, becomes so hot that the parent birds must protect the eggs from the heat of the sun by sitting on the nest, thus covering them. This is done in an exact clock-like rotation every four hours by each bird. It is a constant night and day, day and night vigil accompanied by lively chirps and calls that create such a din, it can be heard even from the deep interior of the fort. The surface of the little island from a distance literally seethes with birds.

As part of an experiment, the ornithologists captured a male nesting gull and confined him aboard the laboratory ship just as it was to return to Woods Hole. The trip took twelve days. When they arrived, he was banded and released. Meantime, observers were watching the female on the nest. When the four hour exchange time came near, she began to look restless and expectant. When the time arrived, she began to call out loudly and urgently. Within half an hour, observers could see that she had been made frantic by his tardiness. Then, as they watched, the whole colony of birds gathered together in council and selected a replacement. They chose a bachelor bird hovering on the fringes of the flock — a spare, so to speak. The substitute seemed more than ready and able to oblige; he was delighted. He settled himself over the egg as though he had helped produce it.

Meanwhile, after two weeks of separation and confinement, the father tern, once released, flew over two thousand miles, from Massachusetts back to the Tortugas, faster than a prop plane could fly in those days. He landed directly beside his nesting spot. His mate refused to give up her place or acknowledge him. Within moments, a signal was given, and the whole flock gathered and then descended on him. He was killed within minutes as a deserter.

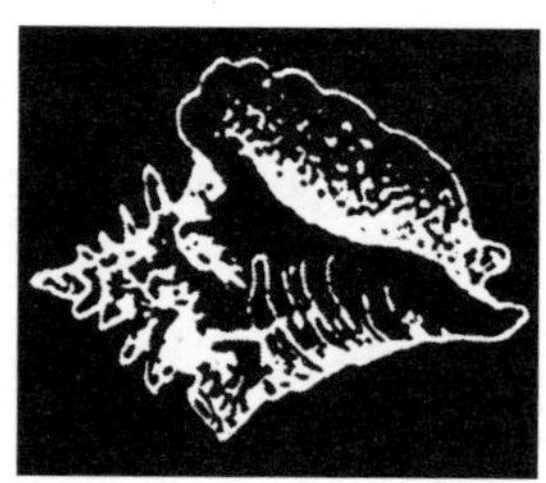

Key West Critters

Raccoons used to abound on the island, but now they have almost disappeared. I miss them a lot, even though they were sometimes a nuisance. They ate a lot of the new green shoots and tasty flowers, and could and did damage the garden. They also had raccoon gang wars held on the roof of the Frost Cottage in the middle of the night. Lying in bed there, one would suddenly hear the rush and frantic scampering of many feet followed by a violent clash directly overhead of two warring tribes. After tremendous ferocity they would retreat to separate parts of the garden to recoup in the greenery and then, refreshed, rush together again amid loud hisses and growls. No one knew the casualty list of wounded and maimed but no one would think of them as fierce territorial battlers either, though they could be and were.

I remember coming in through Heritage House's side garden gate in the evening and glancing up at the arching limbs of our strangler fig tree. A group would be perched there waiting for me and, hopefully, for a carrot handout. They looked as exotic as a collection of Madagacsan lemurs.

The raccoon habit of washing everything before eating it sometimes was their undoing. As children, we would tease them by handing them a lump of sugar. They would take it with relish and delicately hold it down into their water bowl, giving it a bath, while looking up at us greatfully as they did. Then down again to see — nothing! They would comb and swirl the water frantically, look again at their empty hands, holding them up for careful inspection, utterly astonished and bewildered. We thought it was funny, but they didn't.

There are a lot of lizards here still. Several varieties of chameleons, and one little dark-tan fellow with a bright red-tipped tail — all to a degree curious and friendly. Many come indoors to feast on bugs and mosquitoes. Recently a visiting friend seeing one flash across a nearby wall asked astonished, "How did tht baby alligator get in here?" I remember Elizabeth Bishop, the poet, saying she had asked her Conch cleaning lady, "What were all the little black droppings attached to the walls?" And she answered, "Them's lizards."

We also have many varieties of ants here, too, but I won't go into that overcrowded field.

My favorite "critter" story came about recently when a friend, another Jean, house-sitting for a writer and his wife, called me. "You must come and see this phenomenon," she said, "while I'm still here."

The house was located on Love Lane, one of our quaint side lanes in Old Town, with small restored Conch cottages that had once belonged to Key West fishermen. I rode over on my bicycle and was greeted from the screened porch by my friend. She led me through the house and into the master bedroom bath, and without ceremony or explanation she lifted up the lid of the water tank of the john. There sitting on the green copper ball, floating at the top water level, was a handsome medium-sized tree frog. He seemed totally undisturbed or annoyed by his sudden exposure, and he sat observing us candidly, sizing us up and blinking his large dark eyes with an expression of sublime contentment and tranquillity. I, in turn, could hardly believe my eyes.

"We call him Prince John," Jean informed me.

"How in the world does Prince John get in and out of this spot?" I asked in wonder. Then she showed me a rather large hole at the back and top of the water tank.

"That's where he gets in and out," Jean explained. As she said this, she flushed the toilet, and Prince John, totally undisturbed, sank majestically with the descending water that soon erupted at the bottom and began to rise again. The Prince seemed to be enjoying this performance. He had settled himself in against the ball more securely, his long spatulate fingers draped over and holding on against the sides of the ball.

"And that isn't all," continued my friend laughing at my astonishment. "He comes out every evening after sunset, hops over to the sink rim, up here" — she pointed to a higher glass shelf — "then onto the window sill and out the hole made for him in the screen."

"We have seen him outside in the side garden orchid-tarium. He is often joined there by a lady tree frog and they sing together joyfully for a while and then they hop into the bowl of a small fountain for a swim. He always returns before dawn and evidently sleeps most of the day. We feed him occasional fish food that he enjoys and sometimes ant eggs that he adores. Prince John really has a perfect tree frog life — don't you think?"

Sometime soon I want to make this story into a children's book. Please don't anyone steal it.

410 Caroline Street drawing by Wallace Kirke – 1930.
A classic Caribbean colonial sea captain's house c.1834-6.

Oil on the Water

Back in the days when we used well water to save and extend precious rain water caught on our roofs and stored in our cisterns, fresh water was considered almost a holy commodity. Most larger houses had two covered cement cisterns, one beneath the house, the other in the rear or side garden, that could double as a porch or outside dining room on hot evenings. I remember sitting on ours watching moon-flowers growing on a cistern patio arbor trembling open like wet butterfly wings, unleashing a heady and exquisite perfume into the night air.

Well water could be slightly brackish depending on high tides, since we are only about three feet above sea level. It was used for watering gardens or flushing house johns, or for emergencies when the cistern water went down to its last precious inch and blind guppies accustomed to the dark, darted back and forth in the shallows after mosquito larva. When it finally did rain, grateful Conchs would rush out into the streets, arms and tongues extended to welcome and taste every precious drop!.

Our well at Heritage House (410 Caroline Street) and its water, are an important and significant part of Key West history. It was the original outcropping of an underground stream that flows across the Island, and was the original watering spot that attracted first the Indians, later the Spanish, including Ponce de Leon, and then the wreckers and seafarers to the Island. The reason for its prominence and its early use is that it was the water source situated nearest our natural deep water harbor on the southwest side of the Island.

Back in the early 1940s, our well's surface began to mysteriously manifest an

Miss Jessie at the well – 410 Caroline Street

opalescent oil slick that made us sure we were sitting on an oil dome that had opened up geologically under us. Speaking hush-hush to our neighbors, the Garnettes, on Whitehead Street, we found that they, too, were experiencing the same phenomenon with their well. Exciting visions of great potential wealth came with its dark side: ugly oil derricks, black oily sidewalks and wilted gardens. The price for being oil tycoons was just too high, so we kept quiet about the situation for well over a year. I don't know how the news finally leaked out and reached Gladys and Arthur Mulberg who owned the garage and Buick showroom across the street on Caroline. Arthur had been mystified and frustrated for months over the disappearance and loss of valuable oil from his tanks at the far side of his property on Telegraph Lane . . . they showed no outward evidence of leaks. He came over and looked down the dark recesses of our well and saw himself magically transformed in opalescent colors on its surface. "So here is my missing oil!" he said triumphantly as our dreams of empire and wealth faded into oblivion.

*   *   *

Ejection wells into our porous coral rock must be prohibited to save our surrounding waters from pollution.

St. Mary's Star of the Sea Catholic Church

The World is Our Garden

The famous botanist and creator of the Fairchild Gardens, Dr. David Fairchild and his associate assistant, Dr. Gifford often came down to Key West. One morning while we were walking around grandfather Porter's front gardens on Duval and Caroline Street, one of them (I have forgotten which) stooped down and plucked a small weed growing in profusion in the grass "This is the original Hibiscus," he told us. It was a bonsai with serated leaves and several tiny custard yellow flowers that had deep orange magenta centers. They were perfect miniature Hibiscus flowers and can be found all over Key West today. I remember Dr. Fairchild saying that we have wildflowers that are indigenous to Key West and that many of them could be found surviving in the old Key West cemetery.

He said years before a friend of his had stood on the open back caboose of the Florida East Coast Railroad broadcasting seeds of Indian grass off the moving train all the way down the Keys. Indian grass has bright green blades about four inches long that gradates to a bright orangered crimson heart. It then grew all along the railroad bed and later the sides of the roads over the Keys along with Indian daisies that were striped yellow and red with deep magenta centers. I think they too were originally from the wild west. They both survive today on Ft. Taylor's property.

The Keys with their thin topsoil and porous coral rock grew their own bonsai: sea grape and other stunted trees naturally. Betty and Toby Bruce had a wonderful collection of them in their back garden planted in coral rocks.

The Island had many cultivated herbs that Conga Julia used and taught others how to recognize and cultivate. One was Cat's Tongue. It had a leaf that was sharp and pointed and was a low spindly weed about a foot or eighteen inches high. I wish I had paid more attention to herbs cultivated and used here by many Conchs. The reddish thin paper bark of the gumbo limba tree makes a cure-all tea. Everyone had banks of Aloes in there back gardens and used them for everything. One foot long stalk split open could be steeped in a quart bottle of sterile water in the refrigerator for three hours to be drunk and refilled three times using the same stalk. This took care of all stomach problems including cancer and ulcers. We children always put Aloe on sunburns to cool them down and it prevented peeling afterward.

During the WPA days my mother and father asked Jules Stone, the then young administrator: "Why not have workers plant trees along the streets here in town?" He said, "No reason not to if Wallace and Jessie would agree to get up at 6 a.m. and supervise the work.' They did and chose both Poinciana and Honduran Mahogany, varying them from street to street, starting with Whitehead, planting Poincianas there.

Our Poincianas are more beautiful and flamboyant here on the Island then anywhere further north, including Miami. We should celebrate a Pionciana and Bromeliad festival here in May.

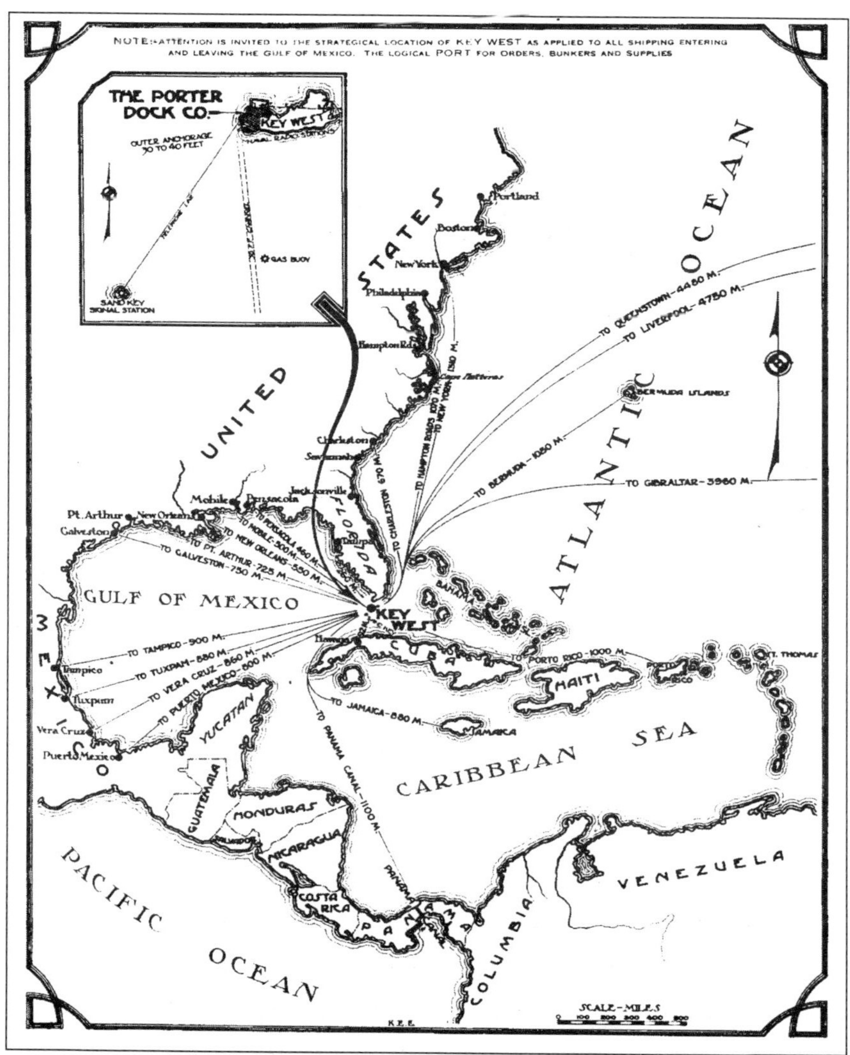

Porter Dock Co. Key West - central location on all shipping lanes as an International Port of Call. W.R. Porter's dream and reality.

The Porter Dock Company

In the past, from all over the world visitors floated or sailed in here to anchor at the Porter Docks at the end of Duval Street.

One morning my grandfather's Vice President, Jerry Trevor knocked, put his head into Pop's office at the bank and said, "Mr. Porter, there's a bum out here who says he's John Barrimore " It was the famous actor, bearded and nautically desheveled looking, just off his yacht docked there. Pop okayed his check and invited him home for lunch. He was delightful company and returned to Key West several times.

Miss Jessie's Old Island Trading Post was part of the Porter Dock property and was located near the water's edge too, where the Pier House gate entrance is now on lower Duval. This building had originally been the ticket office for the Areo Marine Airways, the first overseas commercial airline in the world that started out flying from Key West to Havana.

The big pleasure overnight excursion boats also left from the

Porter Docks. Next to the property manager's house behind the trading post was the pigeon coop that housed Key West carrier pigeons that accompanied the flights to Havana. Wireless equipment was too heavy and bulky in those early days of aviation and was substituted by Key West Carrier Pigeons. If the plane was forced down on the water, they could be released to fly back home to Key West for help and rescue. Fortunately this never occurred I believe. The trading post was raised several feet off the ground above flood water cascading down Duval after heavy rains. I used to launch mahogany pod boats down this rainy season cataract at the corner of Caroline all the way to the end of Duval where it plunged as a waterfall at the Porter Docks into the harbor. The Post was painted a turquoise blue green, one of Mother's favorite colors and had a large bay window displaying ship models and interesting locally hand-made crafts. Its front was sheltered by an overhanging roof of thatched palm fronds that gave it an attractive South Sea island look that lured people in with promise of exotic wares. It was at one time voted the most attractive and interesting small shop in America. The Post is now part of Kelly's restaurant. When my Grandfather sold the Porter Dock properties, Mother moved the building to Caroline and Whitehead where it is now.

Miss Jessie's shop introduced many visitors to Key West with gatherings in the shop's side garden on Sunday afternoons where she would have talented local musicians perform. Key West has always loved and produced wonderful music of all kinds. The old originally blues song, "Love, Oh Love, Oh Careless Love" was written here in Key West in the late 1800s. Why can't we go back to having unamplified music here again - back to the natural which is really Key West style?

Key West Saturday Night

Unlike most Latin towns in the Caribbean, Key West had no central plaza for promenading on Saturday nights. This important social affair had to take place inside the large Kress Dime Store on Duval Street at the corner of Fleming. (Fast Buck Freddy's today) Around the counters, from front to back to front again, the whole town would stroll slowly and purposefully on Saturday nights. Boys and girls flirting and eyeing each other curiously giggling and whispering, and catching each other's eye courting amoratos shooting hot love glances across the counters coming to stand next to each other pretending to select some trinket to touch fingers; young couples feathering their nest with new pillows or pictures or household utensils. All this took place between seven and ten on Saturday night.

Older folk keeping an eye on children and grandchildren would linger over the counters deciding which cologne to buy, Florida water or lemon verbena or some extra luxury they had saved up to acquire on Saturday night.

At Church the next morning they would greet each other: "Where did you buy that lovely brooch Miss Agnes." And Miss Agnes would reply with an air of smug satisfaction, " Twenty five cents to Kress, Ma dear."

Key West ladies serving tea with the Dr. Mudd tea set.
Jessie 2nd from left, Genno Warren, Vivian Pierce &
Connie McLean

The Hemingway House & Garden by Doris Lee

Jeane

McCarthyism
Mme. Nicholi
Angels in the Telephone Booth

Ilean Williams, Minnie Porter Harris, Izzy Bowser, Ann Carlton and Emma Thompson

McCarthyism

Prologue

The nearest I got to being a Communist was accompanying my friend, the poet Kenneth Rexroth, to an Anarchy Party meeting in Berkeley when I was a student there. Our late entrance, and the fact that he was one of their heroes and favorite poets, created such an enthusiastic furor of greeting that it broke up the Anarchy meeting, an irony that didn't escape me at the time. I also went to a Communist meeting in Paris with Pablo Neruda. Picasso was speaking and had just donated his Peace Pigeon propaganda poster "the pigeon that went boom," — his anti-war effort. Picasso's eyes were like the proverbial burning coals; he radiated a special energy and intensity I'll never forget.

Of course, I did have liberal ideas and attitudes — everybody who was in the thinking world (of politics) was a Communist sympathizer. It had become almost a religion in the 30s and 40s: the belief was that if everybody got together and shared what they had and what they needed, we'd all have a much better world. Who could argue with that Utopian idea and not be considered a greedy money grabber? But it was questioned, and with dire results for many people — it became our 20th century witch hunt.

*   *   *

The tall, reedy, neatly tailored woman stood up out of the restless sea of ladies at the Key West Woman's Club meeting. Her voice rang with the quivering intensity of an avenging diva. "I am the mother of five children," she announced, giving her credentials and qualifications for the following diatribe, "and I wish to say that the young woman who is to exhibit her paintings at our Club next week and who went to the University of California at Berkeley, is known to be a rabid communist." She continued after a pause, "I want it on record that I protest the use of this Club by any such individual!"

There was a startled hush among the ladies gathered there that afternoon in January of 1948. The inquisitor, a Navy wife in her late thirties continued, "In addition, I want it known that the artist who is the next in line to exhibit here after this young woman, is a man who also has questionable liberal leanings and is also suspected of being a communist."

The first person on this accuser's black list was none other than myself, and the second was a friend who was then the Key West correspondent for the *Miami Herald*. On a small island like Key West where most everybody knew everybody else, all hell, of course, broke loose. Sides were taken, small contingents were organized, and factions went underground.

My cousin, Minnie Porter Harris, who had been a past president of the Club, got up in indignant fury, pushed down her Lilly Daché straw hat, and walked out of the meeting while the then current president, Emily Goddard, did nothing to control the situation. But stand by.

I had just returned from Berkeley two months earlier to touch home base and hearing about this meeting later that afternoon, I wondered when and if my grandfather would cut off my stipend of $25.00 a month for painting supplies. "Pop" was of the "old school" that believed that too much education ruins a good woman, or at least gets her into trouble. Now here was social support indirectly backing up that opinion as well. Pop was a benevolent despot if there ever was one, who would brook no opposition to his views. "You are not only impudent, Jeane," he would inform me when I'd ask the why of everything, "but the tragedy of it all is," he would continue dramatically, "that you don't even realize you are impudent!" He had always maintained that letting me go to "that Bolshevik California" was the worst thing he had ever let me do. But, although he would question me in private later, he stood staunchly by me publicly.

As it turned out, fortunately for my friend, he was far too good a newspaper man for his paper to question his political leanings on such emotional "evidence" and he kept his job.

I did have my show, which was a success. It was more than just attended, it was packed. Most of Key West had gotten wind of the affair and was there en masse.

And guess who was standing behind the refreshment table helping out by serving humble pie and ladling out punch?

*   *   *

EPILOGUE

Because of this excursion into prejudice, my father and step-mother Wallace and Elanor Kirke, the Garnettes, the Ottos, the Winters, and other interested parties, including myself, joined and supported Joe Allen in starting the Key West Art and Historical Society. I hoped that this would always help insure that Key West would have an open forum to exhibit local and visiting artists' works — in case another McCarthy era threatened to engulf the Island. I was very lucky to escape this Witch Hunt almost unscathed, but many others weren't, all over the country.

Jeane Porter - 1950

Mme. Nicholi

When concerned and helpful friends, seeing my constant dilemma and worry about family property here in Key West, my efforts to have it survive intact and in quality, and struggles to manage it through today's political rapids and rough and changing shoals, say to me, "Why don't you sell it Jeane? Do you really think all this work and worry is worth it?" I remember asking the same question of my appealing friend Mme. Nicholi when I was a young artist in the 50s living in Cagnes Sur Mer, a magic mountain town in the foot hills of the French Alps between Nice and Cannes.

Mme. Nicholi, to put it succinctly, had over-indulged her husband with her wonderful, rich, Provincial cooking. Foie fatigué (liver failure) was endemic to this region and he had died happily , overfed and prematurely in mid-life from her sumptuous cooking.

Her two sons had grown up and graduated from their peasant life of Cagnes and gone off to become commissariats in Nice. They would return every other week or so to do the heavy lifting for her when the produce arrived. But the rest of the time she was left alone with the heavily stocked little grocery store on the village place at the top of the mountain. Every corner and shelf knew her touch and careful attention. I remember her candling a basket of eggs to make sure each was fresh. One day one of her customers searching around in the collection basket announced that he was looking only for the eggs of the brown chicken. "How do you know which are the brown chickens?" asked Mme. Nicholi, taken in with curiosity. "They are the biggest!" informed her customer.

The aroma of her big pot of homemade soup continuously simmering at the back of her store with its provincial herbal scent floating out across the place was an irresistible attraction that still makes my mouth water. Often, she would invite me to share a generous bowl with her. We would sit together behind the counter and sip it while she shared family recipes (trying to teach me to cook) and wisdoms and lamented her lone condition, all this in between attending to customers and exchanging local news with the townspeople.

One day, listening in sympathy, I said to her, "Mme. Nicholi, you have other land that gives you income" — she was the wealthiest peasant land-owner in the region — "and your grocery store would bring you an excellent price on the market. Why, my dear, don't you sell?" Mme. Nicholi sipped a spoonful of her delicious soup, reflected a moment, then shrugged her shoulders philosophically and replied with the down-to-earthness of her practical peasant upbringing . . . . "Would a snail sell its shell?" she answered resignedly. And I guess I agree with her.

Angel in the Telephone Booth

Were you in town in the 40s when *LIFE* magazine asked Miss Jessie to give a 'LIFE GOES TO A PARTY' in her garden in Key West?" asked Martha Sauer. "I think they wanted it to look like Ascot," she continued. "The magazine suggested that we all wear long gauzy chiffon dresses and big picture hats, which we all tried to do. Everybody was there; it was great fun, though certainly not looking typically Key West-ish. The hats kept getting in the way and into the line of vision and into people's eyes and finally we shed most of them." She looked amused remembering, "Do you still have photographs of that party?"

"Yes, I do," I said with pleasure, and I was struck with how suddenly one memory could trigger another strange and fascinating one that had happened so many years earlier.

It was our last evening in New York before flying the next morning for Australia for a three year tour of duty as newlyweds. We had picked out a convenient and pleasant restaurant near our apartment in Tudor City and on a lower concourse across from the

U.N. to say our last good-byes. Parting was more than just sweet sorrow. In spite of the exciting prospect of living in western Australia, it seemed near tragedy to me having to leave my dog behind, a French poodle named Valentina, whom I cherished and adored but could not take with me to that fascinating but restricted country.

The plan was to meet old friends, including the couple who were to inherit my dog, and have one last celebratory dinner before an early morning flight. My mother had come up from Key West to see us off. I had brought Valentina with me, smuggling her past the maitre d' who knew us and turned a blind eye. It was early evening and the restaurant was almost unoccupied. We walked to the back of the room to a large double booth with a large table and my black dog, Valentina, settled in quietly under it by my feet. Looking around, Mother noticed a lighted telephone booth on the other side of the room occupied by a blond, bearded man. To distract me, for she knew I was suffering and trying to conceal my grief, she started to play an old game she had used to amuse me as a child: guessing about the identity and circumstance of an unknown individual.

"He's a British explorer and he is calling his lady friend who is staying at the Plaza," she said. "She's a French Contessa who was with the Underground. They are making plans to meet for dinner." She had not finished her sentence when the light in the booth went off and the man backing out turned in our direction, smiled and came toward us as though Miss Jessie had magnetized him. Indeed she probably had. I had seen my mother produce this magic appeal often, attracting people she wanted to know from across rooms to across continents.

He came over to us smiling, his hand extended in greeting, "Forgive me," he said, addressing Mother, "but I feel I know you. Weren't you the hostess of a LIFE party in Key West a few years ago?"

Mother looked at him both flattered and astonished. That pleasant affair had been over 10 years earlier, but she smiled and extended her hand. He was very attractive, in his late thirties or early forties, with wavy blond hair and a neatly clipped rust blond beard. In the darkened interior of the restaurant he seemed to emit a radiance that surrounded him.

"Why yes," she said and they began to talk — almost like old friends.

He told us that he was a United Nations observer, though it was never disclosed nor did he say exactly for whom. The U.N. at that moment in history (early 1957) was having a crisis of identity and survival and the world was watching, interested and very concerned about it.

The gentleman spoke a British English fluently but as an acquired language, with a slight accent.

At Mother's invitation to join us he settled in delightedly at the table between us and soon became part of the gathering. My memory of the table conversation was blurred. I felt my dog's warmth and presence beside my leg, and knew that these were our last few moments together.

Toward the end of the evening our new blond friend turned to me and touched my arm, his face showing sympathy and concern.

"I know you are suffering," he said, "because you are about to lose something very precious and very dear to you. But don't despair," he whispered, coming closer to my ear, "there is already a replacement that will more than compensate for your loss." I looked at him appreciatively. What a beautiful, kind man he is, I thought, trying to comfort me . . . But replacement? What did he mean I wondered- I had said nothing about my dog to him and she had been quiet and hidden.

Dinner over, farewells and last partings. My Valentina being carried unwillingly into the night. An early morning flight across the continent then across the Pacific to Australia.

Why was I so sleepy? I could hardly keep my eyes open at welcoming dinner parties. Then the rabbit test surprise, "positive," a baby on the way, a son born, a new life begun. Months later I remembered, as I held my son close. He had never replaced my beloved pet but he had certainly more than compensated for the loss of my "best friend."

"Do you believe in angels or visitors from outer space?" I asked my husband. "Do you remember that attractive man we met the last night we were in New York having dinner near the U.N. . . . ?"

Life Magazine goes to a party at
410 Caroline Street - 1938

Ruthie Gailey   *Arlene Printz*

World War 11

Clock Work
Disarming Forces Day
Fortunes of War
The Spy Who Came In From the Heat
Mom's Place

The subtender Bushnell

Clock Work

In the summer of '44 during World War II, when I came home for vacation from college, I worked in the Navy Yard in the Supply Department. The fact that I could type barely fifteen words a minute at the beginning of this venture, and was paid sixty-five substantial dollars a week, infuriated my grandfather, who fumed about government expenditures and waste, and about where taxpayers' money was going.

My job consisted mainly of typing five to seven copies of identical lists of various military hardware acquired, and filing the assorted colored papers in categories — never to be seen again. It all took about one tenth of one percent of the brain that scientists say we only use ten percent of in the best of circumstances. However, this whole experience was enlightening to me on many levels, particularly in the ways of bureaucracy, which I believe is even blinder than blind justice.

My boss and office manager was an attractive young woman, Marguerite Page, who was Wilhelmina Harvey's younger sister. She was professional, competent and tolerant, and her patience and good humor encouraged and inspired me to greater speed by the end of the summer. My desk was very near Marguerite's and we got to know and enjoy each other as friends that summer.

Each day, just before noon, Marguerite's telephone would ring. She would pick it up, pause, check her wrist watch and report the time to the inquirer on the other end of the line. This always happened without fail just before twelve o'clock and became a daily

Inez Poole, Marguerite Page Ecton, Jo Cannon, Sylvia Koenig, Lora Frazier

event falling into the routine of the morning that was broken by the noon whistle.

At noon we all left for a lunch break to picnic on the grass of the administration building or to have a sandwich at the Commissary. Time moved like clockwork — back from one 'til five — with a sea breeze blowing in across the nearby line-up of submarine berths. The big sub tender, Gilmore, was visible on the far knoll like a grim mother machine with all its sharp lethal looking smaller submarine children knifing in and out below us in the harbor.

Toward the end of the summer, just before I was to leave and return to college one morning, Marguerite's phone rang again as expected. It was the voice inquiring the time as usual. For some reason, Marguerite on this occasion thought to ask the identity of the caller.

Sea power in Key West

"Who are you that calls me everyday?"

"I blow the whistle in the Navy Yard at noon," replied the caller.

"Good Lord," gasped Marguerite in horror. "I set my watch everyday by your noon whistle."

It was then that we both realized that the whole Seventh Fleet, and maybe the War, was more or less being run by Marguerite's wrist watch.

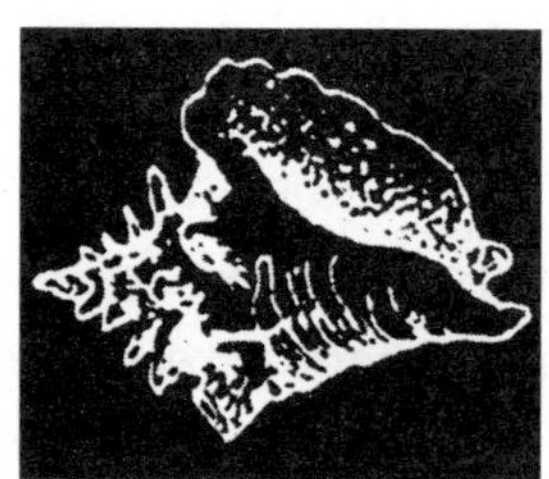

Ernie Pyle and Elmer Davis

I grew up being interested and admiring journalists. Key West has, throughout most of its history, attracted any number of illustrious and famous newspaper men and women— with each of our national wars, strategic military operations were often centered here. During the Spanish American War Arthur Vining Davis and Frederick Remington sat on the front porches of the Jefferson Hotel on lower Duval Street. It was around the corner from the Western Union telegraph office, where they waited for news from Cuba. Since the Hearst boat that was supposed to get them there was unable to make the crossing due to rough weather, they comforted themselves drinking daiquiris and smoking excellent Key West cigars and pretending they were bored. People here who met and invited them over for dinner, the Porters among them, say they didn't look bored at all, and found them very entertaining and genial guests. Marie Capock, the first woman corrospondent ever to cover a war, lived and wrote here. Her journals are kept in the Key West public library perhaps a treasure awaiting discovery.

My memory goes back to just before World World II, with the

press that accompanied the Presidential visits, both Roosevelt's and Truman's. Among them was Ernie Pyle, whom I loved. He came here with his wife on assignment and often visited with us in the 410 gardens in the afternoons. I remember we went roller-skating together at the big rink between Duval and Whitehead on Southard. I was probably about twelve, and Ernie wasn't much taller than I was at that age. He looked like a little exuberant bantam rooster on wheels, soaring and flashing around the rink completely abandoning himself to the music, a mixture of American, jazz, and Spanish tangos, which we both adored. I had a few Cuban Key West boyfriends who tried to keep up with him, but couldn't. He was such an exuberant and joyous little man! A true lover of life.

Elmer Davis was another favorite friend of Miss Jessie's who first came here with FDR's visits. Roosevelt, at the beginning of

Ernie Pyle

World War II, had appointed him head of the Bureau of Strategic Information, which translated into Davis deciding and controlling what important information could and would be released or withheld from the public (i.e. censorship) — a painful assignment for a man who believed so strongly in a free press. Still, he accepted it as a patriotic duty and did it admirably. A good example of information printed in our press before effective censorship: A West Coast newspaper actually stated that the Japanese weren't sinking more U.S. Subs because our subs had the capacity to submerge at least a hundred feet deeper than the Japanese realized and so enemy depth charges weren't reaching them. Voila! This tragic news item changed the odds almost overnight!

When I was attending a Washington D.C. boarding school, Elmer Davis offered to accompany me back there after a Christmas holiday. We were seated on a local puddle-jumper, he on the aisle side craning past me for a better view out the window when the stewardess politely but firmly told us we were to draw the plane's curtains as we were nearing Boca Chica, the huge naval air base. To make sure, she reached past him and pulled down the shade, much to Elmer Davis's chagrin and annoyance, and then his dawning approval when he realized she was just following his orders.

I respected and admired the journalists I knew then because I felt they had a sense of calling and that they believed in and practiced it with much discretion (except for Walter Winchell). They also believed then in the essential individual right of privacy, something we've almost abandoned today, but must rethink.

Disarming Forces Day

rmed Forces Day in late spring was bright and sunny. The whole town turned up on the military beach at the end of Whitehead Street just near the Officer's Club.

Earlier in the day a submarine and a sub-tender, the Bushnell, and a destroyer had been on show and open to the public. I remember looking down a funnel on the aft deck of the destroyer straight into the enlisted men's sleeping quarters below. It was a bit of a shock for a fifteen year old. The view was a voyeur's vision of a sultana's male harem: so many nice pink and white and beige and brown boys all changing into their white starched uniforms getting ready for shore leave!

The crowd moved over to the beach where a team of frogmen was scheduled to perform. I remember Yvonne Snidow, our favorite "touch of Paris in Key West," there in the crowd holding down her large sun-stopping hat while talking to her admirer Admiral Nimitz. Everybody was in flowery dresses and white starched uniforms, and wearing smiles, while a fine breeze blew in

Miss Jessie in her 'native Waters May 31,1960 at Areo Palms in Key West Navy Yard Left to Right: Capt.A. Aleaner-Brazil; Lt CC Mathies - Aids to Rear Admiral John Quinn; on Rt- CA Reid from Panama

from the Gulf. The sky was a light blue with puffs of happy little sheep clouds on the far horizon over the Florida Straits. Someone had even thought to set up an ice cream and soft drink concession for the crowd near the bath house. It was a perfect day for the Armed Forces to show their colors.

As the crowd chatted, a Navy helicopter came buzzing around Fort Taylor Point into view and hovered one hundred yards or so off shore. The gathering could just make out several black-suited scuba divers being lowered quickly into the water where they submerged and disappeared. No one was paying much attention, even when they suddenly reappeared magically on the beach nearby at the water's edge and began clandestinely digging in the sand. Mysterious mission accomplished, they again plunged back into the water and were hauled up into the waiting 'copter which then buzzed back around the point. All was quiet except for the crowd's chatter and laughter as they enjoyed sherbet cones and soft icy drinks and each other. The day was heating up with the sun now almost overhead in spite of a brisk onshore breeze

Suddenly with no warning the whole beach in front erupted, lifting itself up and becoming a ten foot high suspended strata of sand. It hung there horizontally like a mirage, then began to disintegrate from the top down and to blow in sandy chunks inland. With this, the crowd disappeared as though in a London fog, smiles and all, and there followed a total and deafening silence. Gradually, people began to emerge like zombies covered with white sand, mouths open full of sand, eyes full of sand holding sand cones and sand drinks.

No one was hurt fortunately, just overwhelmed and in shock. Needless to say, the event was an impressive Armed Forces Day display of strength that would always be remembered though not, one hoped, ever repeated again.

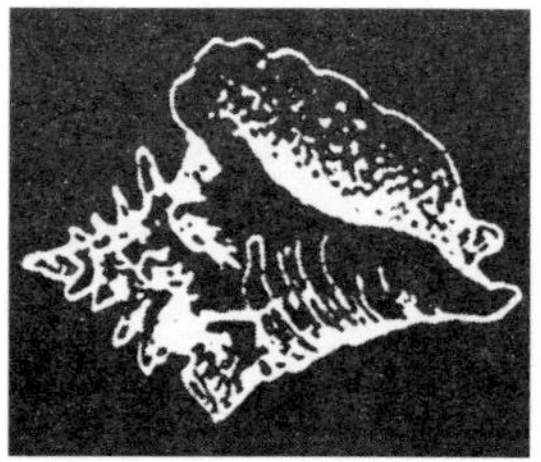

Fortunes of War

The attractive dark-haired square-jawed young man being introduced to me by a friend leaned over my hand in elegant European fashion and said warmly and with enthusiasm, "Ah, so you're from Key West! I remember its lights well." He paused and with a kind of wistful nostalgia and in well-schooled German-accented English continued, "We sat off Sand Key Light for almost three years! The lights at night were most appealing! I remember them well!"

I looked at him with curiosity and then with slowly dawning astonishment as I realized that his view of Key West night life had been not from a terrace but from a German U-boat! The fortunes of war had indeed gone full circle. Here was that "dreaded menace of the deep" materializing at a New York cocktail party as Gerhard Bush, a former German submarine Commander. Here he was, standing before me, a friendly, attractive bachelor, eager and ready to make friends and create a new career and future in the U.S. as an architect.

We sat down with a drink together and began to talk. He told me that as first mate in another U-boat, they had once gone 12 miles up the Mississippi River — this before he had been promoted to captain of the submarine lying off Sand Key.

"Three years," I said in wonderment and looked across the room at my husband, Art Poirier, who had been captain of a submarine chaser during the war. Art, "The Old Man" Captain at twenty-five, was commander of PCS 1419. Every morning at 0600 he and his shipmates, Tom Lasswell and Bob Patten, left the Frost Cottage in 410's (Heritage House) garden and headed for the Navy yard nearby to get their ship underway and out to sea. Submarine chasers were irreverently called the "Donald Duck Flect," a misleading title since they were anything but Disney-esque toys. Armed with deck guns and a hold full of depth charges they headed resolutely and heroically out into waters thick with potential death. German U-boat Wolf Packs, preying on the fringes of convoys and fleets of transports that rendezvoused in the waters off Key West, created havoc for merchant supply ships and their military escort headed for the North Atlantic, England and North Africa all during the war.

Here in Key West, sometimes for weeks at a time, we Islanders couldn't swim in our waters because of the dense seaweed floating in loaded with oil, and the beaches black with tar from freighter sinkings. I remember counting many plumes of black smoke pouring skyward one afternoon alone from ships sighted

Farewell PCS 1419

off Ft. Taylor, that were burning at sea. Often, one could count over twenty ships visible to the naked eye on the horizon while hundreds must have lain in wait to form Atlantic convoys further out over the horizon. Often we were awakened at night with cannons booming from Fort Taylor's batteries on the ramparts and on the dunes, shaking and breaking windows and cracking the plaster ceilings of 410 and in houses all over Old Town.

Anti-submarine warfare was pioneered and developed here in Key West, first by Thomas Edison in World War I. At the beginning of World War II, the sound school was established here where all our allies trained as well. It pioneered equipment and techniques that eventually crippled German submarine activities and won back the control of the Atlantic.

I looked at the attractive young man at my side who would eventually marry my sister's best friend and is still living in Long Island with his family.

"I have someone I want you to meet," I said, beckoning to my husband across the room. "I believe you two were looking for each other!"

Drawing by Wallace Kirke

The Spy Who Came In From the Heat

I f Hitchcock had done the casting as well as the directing, he could not have made a better choice for the part. However, since war is not a game, a play or a movie, it may have proven a fatal one for Nina.

She was a frumpy little woman, plump and square, and suspended somewhere between the age of 35 and 45. She was full of energy and determination, with a middle European accent that was not quite anything one could identify — not Spanish, or German, perhaps Hungarian or Polish? She had a round pale face with dark eyes and black penciled in crescent eyebrows floating high up on a pale white forehead. I don't remember her having eyelashes or perceptible hair since she always wore a turban or snood — made fashionable by films about Morocco and the Casbah starring Heddy Lamar. Snoods were very fashionable for Key West in the hot summer of 1940.

She had met my older cousin, Minnie Porter Harris, while

looking for a place to live. Minnie Porter and her partner Ilean Williams had a successful and perhaps the only official real estate business on the Island then, Old Island Realty. Minnie Porter was also a leading socialite (although she was much too modest and business-like to think of herself as that). She was the current President of the Women's Club, daughter, granddaughter and niece of leading pillars of the community, and a spinster whose considerable energies, having bypassed the channels of marriage, rushed head long and passionately into good deeds and good works, with plenty of energy left over for hobbies. Actually, Minnie Porter excelled in almost everything she put her mind to, especially if connected to God and Country, as the United States teetered on the brink of World War II.

In this instance, Minnie Porter discovered that this frumpy little woman looking for living quarters was in fact a marvelous photographer, particularly gifted in taking family portraits.

It was not difficult for Minnie Porter to find Nina a perfect accommodation, an apartment conveniently and appropriately located for a single woman in the heart of Old Town, situated above Bob Spottswood's drugstore at the corner of Fleming and Simonton Streets. Meantime, her efforts, both hospitable and professional were charged with zeal and enthusiasm to help her new protégé. The two agreed that Minnie Porter's wash house, located in her back garden, be converted into a shared photographic darkroom. In exchange, Nina would teach Minnie Porter her art. My cousin felt it was a marvelous opportunity to learn something new and exciting, as indeed it turned out to be.

For a start, Minnie Porter presented Nina to the Women's Club as a master of family photography. Her new friend's success with club members was immediate. She then introduced her to the Commandant of the Navy yard and his family for photographic sittings that were beautifully conceived and realized. All the Navy followed their lead wearing starched white uniforms, crisp prints, teeth, braces and smiles gleaming, gold epaulets, and buttons polished and hair shining. This was followed in domino style by the entire personnel at the Key West Naval Air Station and at the newly constructed and expanded Naval air station at Boca Chica.

It is accurate to say that most of en famille Key West fell under the spell of Nina's lens during that winter and spring of 1941, while Minnie Porter, with Nina's tutelage, exuberantly documented and pho-

Minnie Porter Harris

tographed our own family in its entirety, photos we all treasured and still have today.

Everything seemed to be clicking along smoothly when one day the U.S. Office of Strategic Services (the CIA at that time had not yet been invented) suddenly arrived and confronted Bob Spottswood, the owner of the building, and together they broke down the locked door of Nina's apartment over his pharmacy. There they discovered what they had suspected: short wave radio sets and apparatus tuned to contact German submarine bases secreted all around the Caribbean. Her extensive photographic collection included graphic details of every military installation on the island as well as Boca Chica. Nina's fate was sealed but is still unknown. She was hauled off in the night without benefit of farewells or good-byes to anyone and was never heard from again.

Poor Minnie Porter, needless to say, was horrified by her own complicity in aiding and abetting a German spy. She completely destroyed and threw away all the darkroom facilities in her wash house. And, unfortunately, she was never ever known to develop another negative.

*   *   *

In the early forties an attractive European couple came into the Old Island Trading post. They said they were Botanists, and that they were studying and documenting seaweeds of the world. Mother found them very interesting and pleasant and invited them to her garden. A few weeks after they had sailed away a government official appeared who was on their trail and told us they were German spies.

Speaking of spies, Hemingway's brother, Jack, wrote a book called "Snoop Cruise through the Caribbean" that came out just before we entered the war in which he named many island bases sympathetic to the Nazis and ready to shelter their ships and subs if and when we declared war.

Jessie, Jeane, Caroline & W.R. Porter - pictures the spy took - 1940

Mom's Place

Hear Ye Hear Ye! Mom's place out Highway 1 to Stock Island turn right at the first light go to the end of the road Is Out Of Bounds!" The young sonorous voice of the Key West Navy radio station announcer would proclaim for the world's and especially for the Navy's benefit. Mom's "Tea Room," as it was fondly called, was the main World War II well-known and "advertised" brothel in the area. It was a rambling Florida bungalow with shady screened porches, set out in the palms and Australian Pines and conveniently located between Key West and the Boca Chica Air Force Base. In the early 40s of World War II, this declaration would be made several times a day over the radio waves.

Half the young men stationed in the Seventh Naval District must have received their beginning sex education and recieved degrees under the friendly tutelage of Mom (Alice ______?). Mom had the familiar warmth and the proverbial flaming red hair of the archetypal Madam. Why this was so I have never quite understood. Perhaps red hair was symptomatic and prophetic fair warning of what was to come after the bliss: Hellfire and damnation? In those nostalgic and seemingly rebellious but relatively innocent days of fading Puritanism, "bad" was generally easy to identify and easier still to label.

Mom's boys, loosed from apron strings and the over-protective and paternal, flocked to the welcoming and comforting arms of Alice and her girls. Everybody loved her. How deeply or personally, I was too young to know at the time, except that Mom would often be seen riding in style down Duval in open convertibles in the middle of our Armed Forces Day parades, and in the company of most of our local dignitaries. She and they always wore very broad smiles while they waved to the crowds. And why not? Anything for, and nothing too good for, our boys!

Navy choir serenading on Heritage House stairs

A Wish List for Key West

1. Southernmost Point Marker

Please, oh, please, replace the Southern most Point marker at the end of Whitehead Street with something we can be proud of. The current one looks like a WW II unexploded bomb and while durable could not be more ugly or sinister looking. It is not what should represent us in photographs taken by thousands of tourist from all over the US and around the world. Better still move the whole thing to the White street pier. I offer this lighted bell bouey tower as a replacement.

2. Mount Trashmore as a Greek Amphitheater

Think of sitting up high on Stock Island ramparts and enjoying a Caribbean-Aegean sunset set to music! That's what could happen from Mt.Trashmore converted into a Greek amphitheater. All that's needed is steel supported concrete steps to sit on to create a half-bowl – and add a stage platform. What a view! Plenty of room for food concessions and parking and a wonderful way to reuse waste space for music, dance, ralleys and fundraisers where noise doesn't matter. Bring on the Spring Breakers!

3. A School of Theater, Radio and Television

Work and productions originating under the auspices of the Florida Keys Community College to be broadcast locally on TV and radio from the college and/or the Tennessee Williams stage, promoted and paid for by local advertisers, businesses and hotels. We have so much artistry and creative talent available here, it is a crime not to use more of it. Key West could become a theater production center with it's own independent Key West productions. It's a natural.

4. Historical Musical Pageant at Fort Taylor

Key West history is as exciting as you can get. Let's make it into an historical musical pageant held on the ramparts and on the parade field of Ft. Taylor. (Interchanging action and audience.) Presented as two historically continuing but separate performances. Begin with the indians using the island as a sacred spot that becomes a battle ground; the Spanish arrive with Ponce de Leon to get water – Ponce calls the keys "Los Marteros," he sees our coral reef formations as supplicant Christians begging for delivery. On to a swashbuckling Juan Salas (who sells the island twice) and introducing Whitehead, Simonton and Fleming; Commodore Porter and Lt. Perry and how piracy was stamped out with Porter's antipiracy fleet. Continue with the heyday of Wreckers 1830-60; William Curry, the Lowes, Hog Johnson and his wife Irene as their King and Queen – Judges Webb and Marvin's court – lighthouse and markers built – The Civil War divides Key West – Union Navy blockade tips scales in favor of North – capture of slave ship –

released at war's end – Key West families reunited – cigar industry booms – The Spanish-American War with the battleship Maine sunk – Teddy Roosevelt and Rough Riders – Remington and Arthur Vining Davis here – Flagler builds railroad to Key West – boom time – cigars depart – Depression starts – sponging blighted – Roosevelt's *New Deal* – artists and writers including Hemingway arrive – WW II – the '35 hurricane – Sound School and Navy here – Truman returns triumphantly to Key West after his election – what a show and what fun!

My Wish most of all;

May our Island develop more perspective so as not to be overwhelmed by commercial successes and greed. .May it preserve its history and retain its outlandish individuality and may it keep a delicate balance intact between vision and reality.

Old Conchs never die, they dry up and blow away.

Jeane at 25 – Key West on Jeane's balconey